T0315822

The Early Modern Englishwoman:
A Facsimile Library of Essential Works

Series I

Printed Writings, 1500–1640: Part 4

Volume 2

Catherine Greenbury and Mary Percy

The Early Modern Englishwoman:
A Facsimile Library of Essential Works

Series I

Printed Writings, 1500–1640: Part 4

Volume 2

Catherine Greenbury and Mary Percy

Selected and Introduced by
Jos Blom and Frans Blom

General Editors
Betty S. Travitsky and Anne Lake Prescott

ASHGATE

Published by
Ashgate Publishing Limited
Wey Court East
Union Road
Farnham
Surrey, GU9 7PT
England

Ashgate Publishing Company
110 Cherry Street
Suite 3-1
Burlington
VT 05401-3818
USA

Ashgate website: http://www.ashgate.com

British Library Cataloguing-in-Publication Data
Catherine Greenbury and Mary Percy. – (The early modern Englishwoman : a facsimile library of essential works. Series 1, Printed writings 1500–1640, Part 4 ; v. 2) 1.Isabel, Queen, consort of Dinis, King of Portugal, 1271–1336 2.Christian saints – Portugal – Biography 3.Queens – Portugal – Biography 4.Spirituality – Catholic Church – Early works to 1800 I.Greenbury, Catherine, 1596–1642 II.Percy, Mary, Lady, 1570–1642 III.Broecke, François van den. Cort verhael des levens, deughden, ende mirakelen IV.Galliardi, Achilles, 1537–1607. Breve compendio intorno alla perfezione cristiana V.Blom, Jos VI.Blom, Frans
282'.092

Library of Congress Cataloging-in-Publication Data
See page vi for complete CIP block

The woodcut reproduced on the title page and on the case is from the title page of Margaret Roper's trans. of [Desiderius Erasmus] *A Devout Treatise upon the Pater Noster* (*c*.1524).

ISBN-13: 978-0-7546-3146-0

Transfered to Digital Printing in 2010

MIX
Paper from
responsible sources
FSC® C004959
www.fsc.org

Printed and bound in Great Britain
by Printondemand-worldwide.com

CONTENTS

Library of Congress Cataloging-in-Publication Data

Paludanus, Frangois, d. 1631.

[Cort verhael des levens, deughden, ende mirakelen, vande H. Elisabeth. English]

Catherine Greenbury and Mary Percy / selected and introduced by Jos Blom and Frans Blom.

p. cm. – (The early modern Englishwoman. Printed writings, 1500–1640, Series 1, Part 4 ; v. 2)

Includes bibliographical references.

ISBN 0-7546-3146-X (alk. paper)

1. Isabel, Queen, consort of Dinis, King of Portugal, 1271–1336 2. Christian saints–Portugal–Biography. 3. Spiritual life–Catholic Church. I. Greenbury, Catharine, 1596–1642. II. Percy, Mary, Lady, 1570–1642. III. Blom, Jos. IV. Blom, Frans. V. Galliardi, Achilles, 1537–1607. Breve compendio intorno alla perfezione christiana. English. VI. Title. VII. Series.

BX4700.I75P35 2006
282.092—dc22
[B]

2006045857

PREFACE
BY THE GENERAL EDITORS

Until very recently, scholars of the early modern period have assumed that there were no Judith Shakespeares in early modern England. Much of the energy of the current generation of scholars has been devoted to constructing a history of early modern England that takes into account what women actually wrote, what women actually read, and what women actually did. In so doing, contemporary scholars have revised the traditional representation of early modern women as constructed both in their own time and in ours. The study of early modern women has thus become one of the most important – indeed perhaps the most important – means for the rewriting of early modern history.

The Early Modern Englishwoman: A Facsimile Library of Essential Works is one of the developments of this energetic reappraisal of the period. As the names on our advisory board and our list of editors testify, it has been the beneficiary of scholarship in the field, and we hope it will also be an essential part of that scholarship's continuing momentum.

The Early Modern Englishwoman is designed to make available a comprehensive and focused collection of writings in English from 1500 to 1750, both by women and for and about them. The three series of *Printed Writings* (1500–1640, 1641–1700, and 1701–1750) provide a comprehensive if not entirely complete collection of the separately published writings by women. In reprinting these writings we intend to remedy one of the major obstacles to the advancement of feminist criticism of the early modern period, namely the limited availability of the very texts upon which the field is based. The volumes in the facsimile library reproduce carefully chosen copies of these texts, incorporating significant variants (usually in the appendices). Each text is preceded by a short introduction providing an overview of the life and work of a writer along with a survey of important scholarship. These works, we strongly believe, deserve a large readership – of historians, literary critics, feminist critics, and non-specialist readers.

The Early Modern Englishwoman also includes separate facsimile series of *Essential Works for the Study of Early Modern Women* and of *Manuscript Writings*. These facsimile series are complemented by *The Early Modern Englishwoman 1500–1750: Contemporary Editions*. Also under our general editorship, this series includes both old-spelling and modernized editions of works by and about women and gender in early modern England.

New York City
2006

INTRODUCTORY NOTE

This volume contains two early seventeenth-century translations of Roman Catholic books by English recusant nuns – one, Catherine Greenbury, a Franciscan, the other, Mary Percy, a Benedictine. To practise their faith on the Continent, both these women, like scores of their co-religionists, fled Elizabethan England, where Roman Catholic practice had been outlawed under pain of severe penalty (even death). While the political and religious situation abroad shifted from welcoming to hostile, and adversity often struck the small, frequently impoverished communities the exiles established abroad, the texts reproduced in this volume (like others reproduced in this facsimile series) bear witness to the success of many of the Elizabethan recusants in surmounting these crosses.

Catherine Greenbury

The title page of the first edition of *A Short Relation of the Life, Virtves, and miracles, of S. Elizabeth* states that the book was translated by 'Sister Catharine Francis'. This was the name in religion of Catherine Greenbury (whose name is also spelled Katharine Greenburie, Greenberie and Greenbery). She was born at York *c*.1595 into a well-to-do upper middle-class family, the daughter of Richard Greenbury and Katherine Dalbie, who is described as a Roman Catholic in 1603 (see Aveling, 1970). Our Catherine married the London silk merchant Rowland Wilcox on 22 December 1613. The marriage resulted in at least one child, a daughter called Marie, born in or around 1616. Within the next few years her husband died, and in the spring of 1620 Catherine Greenbury travelled to Brussels together with her four-year-old daughter in order to take the habit of the Third Order of St Francis. Originally, the Third Order was created by St Francis for laymen, both men and women, who could not – or did not want to – become a Friar or a Sister but nevertheless wanted to live according to Franciscan ideals. However, in the centuries after St Francis's death, the Tertiaries, as they were called, frequently formed religious communities whose members were bound by the three vows of celibacy, poverty and obedience, so that there were not any fundamental differences between their houses and those of the First and Second Orders.

One of the remarkable features of the early seventeenth-century history of the English Catholic community is the explosive growth of convents for female religious. In spite of all the risks and in spite of the near-certain prospect of never seeing England again, many women undertook the hazardous journey to the Continent. Two of them, Lucy Davis née Sleford (c.1566–1638) and Petronilla Brown née Kemp (c.1573–1628), both widows, took the habit of probation of the Flemish Third Order at Brussels in 1619 with the intention of founding an English house as quickly as possible. Petronilla Kemp went back to England in 1620 in order to invite like-minded women to join them. The first person to take up the invitation was Catherine Greenbury. She was clothed on 7 August 1621, together with six other women who had come over in July 1621. Two days later, on 9 August 1621, the convent dedicated to St Elizabeth situated in Buchbore (now Rue des Brigittines) at Brussels was formally inaugurated, with a Flemish nun, Sister Margaret de Castro of a convent at Ghent, appointed as Mother Superior. This arrangement proved to be so problematic that the English sisters threatened to leave the convent if they did not get a superior who spoke English. That is why the Franciscan authorities sent down two English Poor Clares – members of the Franciscan Second Order – from Gravelines in order to lead the young community. The two, Margaret Radcliffe (c.1585–1654) and her sister Elizabeth (c.1587–1645), arrived in September 1622 and restored peace. When in 1626 it was felt that the community was capable of choosing its own superior, Catherine Greenbury became its first elected 'Mother'.

Her subsequent life was very full and very busy. First of all, during her first years as Mother Superior she was translating the biography of Queen Elizabeth of Portugal reproduced on the following pages – it appeared in 1628. Secondly, she had to combine her work for the community with the education of her daughter. From brief statements in the annals of the convent (see Trappes-Lomax, 1922) one gets an idea of her concerns as a mother. Having been brought up in the convent, Marie Wilcox leaves on 30 October 1630 in order to serve the Baroness De Quincy at Douai, but returns on 10 May 1631, because the Baroness has proved to be 'a Right hard ladie' (Trappes-Lomax, p. 18). In spite of this experience she leaves again on 24 October in order to serve Lady Babthorp at Antwerp. We do not hear anything about the success of her service, but the next reference to Marie in the annals is on 5 April 1633, when she takes the habit of probation at the age of 17 and a year later makes her profession 'in the hands of the reuerend Mother Sister Catherine Francis Abbesse of this Cloister ... & naturall mother of the forsaid Mary' (Trappes-Lomax, p. 134). And thirdly, Catherine's work as an Abbess must have been very demanding. In 1628 she supervised an alteration and extension of the convent made necessary by a rapid increase in the number of sisters; by 1626 the convent housed 34 nuns. In 1635 she guided the community through a plague epidemic during which five nuns and the father confessor died. And two years later she organized the transfer of the convent from Brussels to Nieuwpoort: the house had become too small and provisions at Nieuwpoort were less expensive. On 21 November 1640 Catherine resigned her office. She died on 17 February 1642 at the age of 46; her obituary mentions the 'great zeal and exempler virtue' with which she 'most laudably governed with example of all pietie and deuotion, humility and zeale of her holy profession the space of fifteene years' (Trappes-Lomax, p. 181).

A Short Relation of the Life, Virtves, and miracles, of S. Elizabeth

The book that Catherine Greenbury translated, extant in only one known copy belonging to the Ruusbroecgenootschap at Antwerp, was a work in Dutch entitled *Cort Verhael des Levens, Deughden, ende Mirakelen, vande H. Elisabeth ... Coninginne van Portvgael* (Antwerp 1625), written by the Flemish Franciscan François van den Broecke (d. 1631), also known as Franciscus Paludanus. Basing himself on a number of historical accounts van den Broecke compiled a French, a Spanish and a Dutch life of the saintly Queen Elizabeth of Portugal (1271–1336), who was canonized on 25 May 1625; publication of van den Broecke's texts was clearly meant to coincide with the festivities accompanying this event. An additional reason for van den Broecke to write her biography was Elizabeth's connection with the Franciscans: she herself had joined the Third Order, had donated considerable sums to Franciscan convents, and was buried in the Poor Clares' house at Coimbra, Portugal – still a place of pilgrimage in her honour. As the introductory note to another volume in this series explains (see Blom and Blom, 2002a), at this time the Franciscans were concerned to prove how important their order had been in the history of the Catholic Church. The book itself is traditional hagiography, cramming as many virtuous acts, wonderful qualities and miracles into its pages as possible. A representative detail is the story about how Elizabeth was surprised by her husband when taking alms to the poor (a story also told about Elizabeth of Hungary [c.1207–31]). When the husband insists that she show what she is hiding under her mantle the gifts are miraculously changed into roses.

Catherine Greenbury's decision to translate the life was obviously related to Elizabeth's Franciscan sympathies, but it remains remarkable that she chose to translate from the Dutch rather than from the French, command of which was much more common among contemporary English people. The information that she translated from the Dutch is given in a dedication by the later martyr, the Franciscan Arthur (in religion Francis) Bell (1590–1643), from 1623 to 1630 confessor at the convent. In this dedication he tells us that he found the manuscript in Catherine Greenbury's hand, presumably meant only for the use of the other members of the convent, and decided that it had to be printed 'for the commun good'. The title page makes it clear that he took the manuscript to the Brussels printer Jan Pepermans, who also printed three of Bell's own books (see Allison and Rogers, 1994), two of which likewise concern Franciscan subjects. Bell's preface was followed by a second one, fortunately available to Catherine Greebury, 'The author to the reader', but curiously absent from the only extant copy of the original. This 'authorial' comment by van den Broecke does not say anything about the present book, but it does advertise one of his other publications, a one-page genealogical chart (van den Broecke, 1626) proving that among the descendants of Elizabeth were not only 24 saints but also '7. Emperours, consequently one after another: six Empresses: 36. Kings: and 43. Queenes'. Apart from the fact that such an illustrious progeny adds to the glory of the saint, the writer's main political point seems to be that Philip IV is the rightful heir to the kingdoms of the greater part of Europe and that it would be sacrilege to take away from him what God has given.

A line-by-line comparison of Greenbury's version with the Dutch text shows that the translation is very competent and very faithful, but also that she takes the editorial freedom to improve the text. She leaves out certain details, presumably because she did not consider them important (for example, the facts that Elizabeth was born with a caul and the preservation of this caul); she inserts summaries to make the long sentences of the original more intelligible (for example, on page 6 'all which were motives that made the king her father willing to bestow her upon the aforsayd king Dionysius'); and at times she demonstrates her independence (thus at the top of page 35, whereas the Dutch had stated that after her husband's death Elizabeth did not indulge in typically female weeping, the English has 'she made not much shew exteriourly'). The mistakes that occur mostly concern commas and full stops in wrong places: for example, after line 5 on page 7, where the word 'heaven' ought to end the sentence. Perhaps these mistakes are by the compositor, not by Greenbury. Evidence that the compositor did not have any English is provided by spelling mistakes such as 'à side' for 'aside' (sig. A7^r, 13th line from the top). We do not list these minor errors, since they do not cause confusion.

There is only one extant copy known of Greenbury's translation, now at The British Library. The title page bears the name of the first owner, Elizabeth Radcliffe. (As was pointed out above, Elizabeth and her sister, Margaret, were in charge of the convent until the Brussels nuns could cope for themselves.) The other name on the title page is that of John Morris (c.1580–1658), the wealthy book collector whose library has been described and analysed by Birrell (1976).

Lady Mary Percy

The dedicatory epistle to the first edition of *An Abridgment of Christian Perfection*, a translation of *Breve Compendio Intorno alla Perfezione Cristiana*, is signed 'P. M.'. These are the initials of Mary Percy, an

English Benedictine nun at Brussels. Decisive evidence for the identification is provided by a manuscript, now at Downside Abbey (shelfmark D.4) and quoted in Allison (1957). It was written by a contemporary of Percy, the Benedictine mystic Augustine Baker (1575–1641; see also below). Referring to *Breve Compendio*, he states: 'In the year, 1612, it was translated, and set forth in English by & under the name of the Lady Mary Piercy, then and now Abbesse of Brussels'.

Mary Percy was born in 1569 or 1570, one of the four daughters of Thomas Percy, seventh Earl of Northumberland (1528–72) and his wife Anne Somerset (d.1591). Thomas Percy, whose family had very ancient roots in the north of England (cf. Shakespeare's *Henry IV*) and who had remained faithful to the old religion, was executed in 1572 for his part in the ill-advised rebellion of the northern earls in 1569. His widow fled abroad, leaving her children in England. At a later stage Mary also left the country and went to Flanders, where she felt attracted to a religious life. She first spent some time with the Flemish Austin Canonesses, but this appeared not to be a satisfactory option, so together with Dorothy Arundell (*c.*1560–1613) and her sister Gertrude (*c.*1571–1636), Percy decided to found a Benedictine convent especially for Englishwomen. In 1598 she bought a house in Brussels, found an experienced nun (Lady Joanna Berkeley [1556–1616] from Rheims) to become the first abbess, and managed to attract the interest of influential patrons such as the Archduke Albert and Archduchess Isabella, rulers of the Spanish Netherlands. The new foundation, named the Convent of the Assumption of Our Blessed Lady, was officially started on 14 November 1599 with the appointment of Lady Joanna Berkeley as abbess, and the next year Mary Percy made her profession. This convent was the first of more than twenty houses for English nuns established in the seventeenth century, and it was directly or indirectly involved in the foundation of five other communities of English Benedictine nuns on the Continent (Cambrai [1623], Ghent [1624], Paris [1651]), Boulogne [1652] and Dunkirk [1662]).

In 1616 Mary Percy became abbess, and under her rule the convent prospered. The number of nuns grew rapidly, the house's finances were sound (always a difficult issue for convents depending on dowries and donations) and the Infanta Isabella became Percy's personal friend (Arblaster, 1997). However, Percy's period as abbess was also marked by a long drawn-out conflict that deeply divided the sisters. The conflict concerned the choice of a confessor. All convents had confessors, who were responsible for the spiritual guidance of the nuns and who thus exerted great influence on the spiritual life of the community. The archbishop of Mechlin, under whose authority the convent was placed, at first appointed a secular priest as confessor, but when some of the nuns were unhappy with this appointment they were allowed to have their own Jesuit director. Thus the problems between seculars and Jesuits that were a feature of the history of the English Recusant community at this time were imported into the convent, and it took until 1636 for the dust to settle. Many different factors played a part in the conflict, ranging from politics to clashing personalities (see Pasture, 1930–32, and Guilday, 1914, for extensive documentation), but one of the issues was the kind of spirituality that was to be practised. With regard to the latter, the pro-Jesuit party argued for the method laid down in the *Spiritual Exercises* (1548) by Ignatius of Loyola, the founder of the Society of Jesus, while a less methodical, more contemplative and mystical spirituality was advocated by the anti-Jesuits.

At first Lady Mary Percy seems to have been firmly pro-Jesuit. However, when a number of nuns refused to accept anyone except a real Jesuit as confessor, tensions ran so high that in 1623 three nuns were sent to the new Benedictine foundation at Cambrai (which immediately experienced the same problems as at Brussels), and in 1624 most of the pro-Jesuit party moved out in order to found a house of their own at Ghent. (See Lunn, 1980, and the introductory note to Deacon, in Blom and Blom, 2002b.) By this time Mary Percy's sympathies for the Jesuits had considerably cooled, especially when it turned out that the situation at Brussels had not permanently improved. When in 1628 a new chaplain, the secular priest Anthony Champney (1569–1644), was appointed, nineteen out of the fifty-five nuns refused to submit themselves to his direction. The conflict escalated to such an extent that in the course of the next ten years many people from outside the convent got involved, from laymen and lower clergy to papal nuncios, the Archbishop of Mechlin, cardinals and even the Pope in Rome. The conflict clearly demonstrates Mary Percy's determined character and temper – she was after all a descendant of Hotspur. She saw the matter in the light of holy obedience and monastic constitutions and did not want to sacrifice her confessor.

Eventually a compromise was found by which the rebels would withdraw to a house nearby while Champney remained the confessor of those who decided to stay. By the time that Champney got another post in 1637, the rebels had gradually returned to the convent and formally made their submission to the abbess, as Percy had demanded. Mary Percy died in 1642.

An Abridgment of Christian Perfection

In the light of the conflict about the merits of Jesuit spirituality described above, Mary Percy's involvement in the translation of *Breve Compendio Intorno alla Perfezione Christiana, dove si Vede una Prattica Mirabile per Unire l'Anima con Dio* is remarkable. The book is variously attributed to the Italian Jesuit Achille Gagliardi (1537–1607), sometimes spelled 'Galliardi', and to the saintly Milanese Lady, Isabella Berinzaga (*c.*1551–1624), sometimes spelled 'Bellinzaga'. Gagliardi completed the usual stages of Jesuit training in Rome and Turin, made his solemn profession in 1575 and had filled several posts in the order when, at the special request of Archbishop Carolus Borromeus, he was transferred in 1580 to Milan, where he stayed for fourteen years. His functions were many: he worked as confessor and preacher, became superior of the Jesuit House of San Fedele, and wrote a catechism together with Borromeus. It was here that he came into contact with Isabella Berinzaga, who had already gained a reputation for piety and mystical spirituality with religious leaders such as Borromeus and the Jesuit General Mercuriano. In 1584, when she sought spiritual guidance from the Jesuits of San Fedele, Gagliardi became her spiritual director. Theirs proved to be a fruitful co-operation, although not an unproblematical one. Gagliardi saw in Berinzaga an ideal means to test his ideas about spirituality.

The result was *Breve Compendio*, probably completed in 1588. With regard to its authorship one might posit that, on the face of it, it would seem more likely that it was written by the spiritual director than by his student. However, there is conflicting evidence. On page 148 of the text the statement 'Whilest I was writing a copy of this booke, our Lord made this virtuous dame that composed it to vnderstand that she should aduertise me of this that followeth ...' suggests that Gagliardi was the editor rather than the author. The issue is further complicated by the fact that as early as 1588 Gagliardi was accused of unorthodoxy by fellow Jesuits, who also entertained suspicions about his close relationship with Berinzaga. It was 1601 before the matter was rather half-heartedly settled by Pope Clement VII, and in the meantime it was in nobody's interest to be too explicit about the work's authorship. Most probably the book came into existence as a collaborative effort by Gagliardi and Berinzaga, with Gagliardi drawing up the programme and giving the book its final shape and Berinzaga reporting on her experiences.

As a result of the controversy surrounding *Breve Compendio* the Church authorities decided that it would be better to put an end to the relationship between Gagliardi and Berinzaga. In 1594 Gagliardi was transferred from Milan to Cremona and then to Brescia. He ended his career as Superior of the Jesuit House at Venice, where he died in 1607. Apart from the works mentioned above, he left a number of manuscripts behind, among them a commentary on the *Spiritual Exercises*. Isabella Berinzaga spent the rest of her life quietly 'like a good servant of God'. She died in Milan in 1624.

Perhaps it is not so surprising that objections against the book came from members of the Society of Jesus, since the *Breve Compendio* is a mystical handbook and is much closer to the ideas incorporated in the works of the Benedictine Augustine Baker (mentioned above) than to those of the *Spiritual Exercises*. In commenting on the book, Baker, who was teaching the ways of mysticism to the Benedictine nuns at Cambrai – among them his star pupil, Gertrude More (1606–33) – loudly argues that in view of its contents it could never have been written by a Jesuit. As readers of Percy's translation will see, the pillars upon which the *Breve Compendio* rests are a sense of one's own utter worthlessness and of God's supreme greatness. The person aspiring to perfection is led through a series of elaborately defined stages (here called 'estates' and 'degrees') to a state of complete indifference in regard not only to such worldly affairs as status or health but also to such spiritual matters as divine consolation and even reward in Heaven. The candidate is warned that he or she can expect periods of profound darkness, frustration and despair; these periods, however, will be steps on the road to the destruction of every shred of 'self-love'. Quite often the authors demonstrate their psychological insight by showing that renunciation is frequently accompanied by secret satisfaction about one's own ability to renounce matters, and the lesson again is that this satisfaction makes it impossible to reach perfection. The summit towards which one strives is called 'deiformitie', a state in which the soul is 'vnited vnto the will of God, and so transformed into the same, that now it seemeth not to be her will that worketh, but the will of God which worketh in her: as though she had giuen her owne hart vnto Christ' (sig. *6v). For many modern readers it is difficult to judge – or even form a picture of – this ideal, but the present editors have to admit that they felt disturbed by the gloom that seems to hang over much of the book.

As far as the actual translation is concerned, the title page of the first English edition (1612), reproduced in the following pages, tells us that the book was translated out of French: because of problems with regard to the orthodoxy of the treatise there were no Italian editions before 1611. However, the *Breve Compendio* circulated in manuscript, was translated into French, and was published in a number of different French editions from the end of the 1590s onwards. The third preface of Percy's translation, entitled 'To the soules truly united unto God', written by 'D.C.M.', an unidentified French editor, and dated 'Paris, this thirteenth of Iuly 1598', states that the original French translation contained many errors and that a corrected Paris edition was brought out in 1598. It is that edition, or one of its reprints, that Mary Percy translated: no copies of the Paris edition seem to have survived, but the Catholic University of Louvain possesses a 1599 Arras reprint (see *Discours*), which on inspection indeed proved to be the original text from which Percy worked. From Baker we further hear that Percy was assisted by the Jesuit Anthony Hoskins (1568–1615), who was residing at Brussels at the time. Hoskins apparently translated the 'To the reader' and helped see the work through the press.

Apart from translating the body of the text, Mary Percy also wrote the first preface 'To the Religiovs of ovr Nation', that is, to the other English nuns who were living in convents on the Continent. It is a lucid, well-written piece in which she first of all warns the general reader that the path to perfection described in the book will not be open to everyone: it will be profitable only for those whom God has 'called ... from the pursuite of worldly vanities'. Her fellow sisters are obviously people who qualify in this way and for them she describes in glowing terms what the rewards of this rigorous pursuit of perfection will be. One of her concerns in the preface is to explain in simple terms the complicated concepts that play a key role in this mystical handbook. For that purpose she develops an extended metaphor concerning digging for a treasure that has to be found, cleansed and purified. The preface in any case impresses upon the reader the writer's strong personal involvement with the essence of the *Abridgment*.

In 1625 the *Abridgment* was brought out again, this time by the Jesuit-oriented English College Press in St Omer. The translation is virtually the same as the one published in 1612, but nevertheless there are some remarkable changes in the volume. The title page states that the book was written by 'Fa. Achilles Galliardi of the Society of Jesus, & translated into English by A.H. of the same Society'. Presumably by 1625 the book had become so popular through its Italian, French and Dutch editions that the overseer of the English College Press, John Wilson, thought that it would be advantageous to claim both the book and its English translation for the Society. In naming the author he may have felt justified by the appearance of a French edition in 1612, edited and translated by the prolific French Jesuit author Etienne Binet: the title page of that edition was the first to name Gagliardi as its author. With regard to the English translator there was no justification at all. In order to make his ascription plausible, Wilson had to tamper with the text, and so he did. Mary Percy's preface 'To the Religiovs of ovr Nation' now starts off 'This little booke (devout religious in Christ Iesus) being first written in Italian by the R. Father Achilles Galliardi of the Society of Iesus, and delivered over, in printed papers only, unto an honourable and very devout Lady of Milan, for her private instruction ...' . The rest of the preface remains the same, but the initials 'P. M.' are changed into those of Anthony Hoskins. The phrase on page 148, quoted above, about the 'vertuous Dame that composed [the book]' had to be changed too and runs in the 1625 edition 'whilst I was writing a copy of this booke, our Lord inspired this vertuous Dame for whom it was first composed ...' and when one compares the text of page 141 of the present edition with that of Wilson's version one also finds the pronoun 'she' consistently changed into 'he'. The second edition had three more issues after 1628 (see Allison and Rogers, 1994); in two of them, credit for the translation reverts to Mary Percy.

There is only one copy of the first edition, at the English College, Rome. It was mislaid half a century ago, so that Allison in his 1957 article on Percy's translation had to rely on a transcript, not the actual book. Fortunately it was recovered recently, just in time for the present edition. The manuscript notes on the half title and on the actual title page suggest a fascinating provenance. The Latin text on the half title ascribes the book to Galliardi and states that it was published under his name at Brescia, Viterbo and Naples. The top and bottom lines of the manuscript text on the title page suggest that the copy originally belonged to the English Jesuit house at Liège and was subsequently sent to the English College at Rome. The line in the middle is hard to decipher but might read: 'Cubiculo P. Carafae pro orig.'; that is to say: 'The original text is in the study of Father Carafa'. Vincent Carafa was the Jesuit General. In 1637 he appointed as his secretary the English Jesuit Nathaniel Bacon *alias* Southwell (1599–1676), who was at the time Minister and Procurator at the English College, Rome, and who may have continued to live there after his appointment. Southwell's fame rests on the massive Jesuit bibliography that he published in 1676 under the title *Bibliotheca Scriptorum Societatis Jesu*. In this bibliography the English translation of *Breve Compendio* is mentioned under the name of Anthony Hoskins, while the name of the original author is omitted. The bibliographical expertise in the manuscript notes, together with the Carafa connection, makes it very tempting to speculate that the only extant copy of Percy's translation is at the English College because Carafa was worried about the book's orthodoxy and therefore requisitioned the English version from Liège. Since his secretary, Southwell, was English, it was logical that the latter would keep the copy, and since he lived at the English College Rome it is still there.

Acknowledgement

We thank Sister Mary Joseph, librarian at the English College, Rome, for cheerfully undertaking a successful search for the unique copy of *Abridgment* housed there.

References

STC 19167 [*A Short Relation*]; *STC* 11538.5 [*Abridgment*]

Allison, A.F. and D.M.Rogers (1994), *The Contemporary Printed Literature of the English Counter-Reformation between 1558 and 1640*. Volume II: Works in English, Aldershot: Ashgate

Allison, Anthony (1957), 'New light on the early history of the *Breve compendio*. The background to the English translation of 1612', *Recusant History* 4.1: 4–17

Arblaster, Paul (1997), 'The Infanta and the English Benedictine Nuns: Mary Percy's Memories in 1634', *Recusant History* 23.4: 508–27

Aveling, J.C.H. (1970), *Catholic Recusancy in the City of York 1558–1791*, Publications of the Catholic Record Society, Monograph 2, London

Bibliotheca Sanctorum (1961–69), Istituto Giovanni XXIII della Pontificia Universita Lateranense, Rome

Birrell, T.A. (1976), *The Library of John Morris*, London: The British Library

Blom, J. and F. Blom (2002a) *Elizabeth Evelinge II*, The Early Modern Englishwoman: A Facsimile Library of Essential Works, Printed Writings 1500–1640, Series I, Part 3, Vol. 5, Aldershot: Ashgate

Blom F. and J. Blom (2002b), *Pudentiana Deacon*, The Early Modern Englishwoman: A Facsimile Library of Essential Works, Printed Writings, 1500–1640, Series I, Part 3, Vol. 4, Aldershot: Ashgate

Discours de l'abnegation interieure avec un abregé de la perfection Chrestiènne où sont contenuz & compris plusieurs beaux enseignements preceptes & advertissements touchant la saincte & sacrée theologie mystique. À Arras, de l'imprimerie de Guillaume de la Rivere. 1599 (copy at Louvain)

The Franciscan Experience, www.christusrex.org/www1/ofm/fra/FRAmain

Guilday, Peter (1914), *The English Catholic Refugees on the Continent 1558–1795*, London: Longmans & Co.

Hansom, Joseph S. (ed.) (1914), 'The English Benedictine Nuns of Brussels and Winchester, 1598–1856', *Miscellanea IX*, Publications of the Catholic Record Society, Vol. 14, London

Lunn, David (1980), *The English Benedictines 1540–1688*, London: Burns & Oates

Majérus, Paul (2001), *Ordres Mendiants Anglo-Irlandais en Belgique*, Brussels: Archives Générales du Royaume

Oxford DNB (2004) s.v. Mary Percy

Pasture, A. (1930–32), 'Documents concernant quelques monastères anglais aux Pays-Bas au XVIIᵉ siècle', *Bulletin de l'Institut Historique Belge de Rome*, Vols 10–12

Thaddeus, Father (1898), *The Franciscans in England, 1600–1850*, London and Leamington: Art & Book Co.

Trappes-Lomax, Richard (ed.) (1922), *The English Franciscan Nuns 1619–1821 and the Friars Minor of the Same Province 1618–1761*, Publications of the Catholic Record Society, Vol. 24, London

Van den Broecke, François (1625), *Cort Verhael des Levens, Deughden, ende Mirakelen, vande H. Elisabeth, de Vredsamighe Ghenaemt; Coninginne van Portvgael, Huysvrouwe des Conincx Dionysii, vanden Reghel S. Francisci der Penitentie. Ghecanoniseert van den Teghenwoordigen Paus Urbanus den VIII anno 1625 den 25 Maij. Ghetrocken uyt Verscheydene Historieschrijvers*, T'Antwerpen bij William Lesteens in de hoochstrate inden gulden Pellicaen

———— (1626) [Genealogy of the House of Austria.] *Invictissimis ... Imperatori sacratissimo, Regi Monarchæ maximo. heroinis inclitis Austriacis. Potentia, armis, ... Orbi Christiano, prælucentibus. A. S. Elisabetha Lusitaniæ regina ... in nono decimo, rectæ lineæ descendentis gradu, progenitis: cæteros sanctos (quorum effigies hoc scema exhibet) cognatione, ac affinitate, gradibus hic conspicuis, attingentibus. F. P. ... d.d. (S. vanden Schore sculpsit et excudit*, Brussels (copy at BL]

www.familysearch.org

JOS BLOM AND FRANS BLOM

A Short Relation of the Life, Virtves, and miracles of S. Elizabeth (*STC* 19167) is reproduced, by permission, from the copy at The British Library, London (shelfmark 701 a 5[2]). The text block measures 123 × 66 mm.

A
SHORT RELATION,
OF THE LIFE, VIRTVES,
and miracles, of

S. ELIZABETH
CALLED THE PEACE-
MAKER.
QVEEN OF PORTVGALL.

Of the third Rule of S. Francis.

Canonised by Pope VRBAN the VIII. the 25. of May. Anno 1625.

Translated out of Dutch; by Sister
Catharine Francis, Abbess of
the English Monasterie of
S. Francis third Rule
in Bruxelles.

IOHN MORRIS.

AT BRVXELLES,
By Ihon Pepermans, at the signe of
the goulden Byble, 1628.

S.ELIZABETHA PORTVGALLLÆ REGINA
tertij Ordinis S. Francisci Vixit annis LXV. Obijt an. 1336.
Sculp: et Exaud: St. Van Schere

TO THE REVEREND,

SISTER CATHARINE

FRANCIS,

Abbess of the English Monaf-
terie of S. Francis third
Rule, in Bruxelles.

Euerlafting health.

REVEREND MOTHER.
Having feen in English
the little booke of the
life of S. ELISABETH Queen of
Portugall : vvhich F. Paludan.
abbridged, and gaue out to all
the people in Spanish, French,
and Dutch, in the folemnitie made at the publishing of her Ca-
nonifation, in Bruxelles: I knew
it to be your Reuerences hand
wrighting, and being farder cer-
A 2   tified

tified that it was your ovvne labour, and that you had your felfe tranflated it out of the dutch. Efteeming it fo much the more, I conferred it with the originall; and finding it in all things to agree, and to be à mirrour, not only for Religious, but alfo for Princes, I had fcruple to hide vvhat vvas fo behouefull for the commun good; therfore witneffing heer the truth of the tranflation, I demaded of our fuperiour his approbation that it might be printed, vvhich had, I dedicate your worck to your ovvne felfe, vvilling you to go forvvard in fo good exercife, for nothing moveth more to perfection then the examples of thofe faintes that vvere in all refpectes of the fame profeffion that our felves are: nor contrarievvife can any thing more hinder it, then to be bound to one profeffion, and

in

in affection to follovv another. Verely, to your ferious looking into theyr liues (next vnto your dayly, and nightly exercife of quire and meditation) I muft attribute that principall fpirit of gouernement, to vvhich in short time you haue attained by the affiftance of him who needeth no long times in teaching, Almightie God, who euer blefs your endeavours, and bring vs all to fee his face, in heaven. Pray for your pore Chaplain.

BR. FRANCIS BEL.

A 3　　　THE

THE AVTHOR, TO
THE READER.

TVrning ouer diuers Authors, and with attention reading theyr histories, the better to informe my selfe of the parentage, affinitie, and life of our holy Queen Elizabeth: I haue found that her Origen is the illustrious howse of Aragon, and her alliance by mariage, with the kingly howse of Portugall, which howses I haue noted to haue been very fruitfull of holy persons: And not only in thees two but also in many others, as France, Castile, Bohemia, Hungarie, Poland, and Brabant I haue obserued the like blessings and fauours. Amongst which kingdomes and Princedomes, the mutuall mariages and alliances from all antiquitie, by course even till this time haue caused an affinitie worthie the consideration: In

ſo

ſo much that the Princes and Potentates liuing this day, if they bee come
of thees familıes, haue either theyr
origen from the number of thees
Saintes or elles are allied and of kin-
red to them reigning now in glorie
with Chriſt our ſauiour.

Chiefly it is to bee noted how this
holy Saint Eliſabeth Queen of Portugall is Parent to the Emperour Ferdinand, the 2. and the Catholique
King of, Spaine Philip Dominicus
victor, by right line in the tenth degree. To the Infanta Iſabella Clara
Eugenia, gouerneſs of the lowe countries and Burgondie, in the 9. degree. To the Duke of Bauaria and
the Duke of Nuburg, in the 11. degree.

The moſt Chriſtian King of France,
that now liveth, is to her and S.
Lewes, his predeceſſor in the kingdome of France (who was alſo of the
third Order of our Seraphicall father
S. Francis) and to her Siſter S. Eliſabeth

beth *who was à Nunne of S. Clares Order*; *in the eleventh degree: he is also cozen to S. Lewes Bishop of Tolosa, who was à Freer of S. Francis Order*: *and also to B. Ioanna Queen of France, Foundresi of our B. Ladies order, called the Anuntiates.*

The King of Poland *that reigneth at this day*, hath in his Parentage S. Hedwigis, and her daughter. S. Gertrude; and B. Aleyda Princesi of Poland, and B. Salomea Queen of Halicia, Moreover, he hath S. Casimirus, his uncle, Brother to his grandfather.

The Lantsgraue *of Hessen descendeth from* S. Elisabeth Queen of Hungarie and Bohemia (shee was of the third order of S. Francis) hee is in the 10. degree from her.

The kingdomes of Hungarie and Bohemia haue honored theyr kings and Princes with parentage of Saints and Beatified, Saint Elisabeth before mentioned, and S. Margarite (of the order of S. Dominick) Cunegunda and

and *Iolenta* of the order of *S. Clare* :
all daughters of *Andrew* the 3. and
Bela the 4. *Kings of Hungarie*: *B. Ag-*
nes of the order of *S. Clare* daughter
to *Primiſlaus king of Bohemia: S. Al-*
bertus Cardinall and Martyr *Bishop*
of *Leedes* (whoſe reliques ly in *Bru-*
xelles in the church of the *Diſcalced*
Carmelites , tranſlated thither from
Rhems by the *Archduke* of happy me-
morie *Albertus* the *Iuſt*, and *Iſabella*
Clara Eugenia his beloued wife the
year 1612.) who was ſonn , brother ,
and vncle to the *Dukes of Brabant.*

But heer I deſire you to marck, how
the kingdome of *Portugall*, goeth be-
yond the others ; for ſetting aſide the
holy *Eliſabeth* (whoſe life ſhall heer
briefly bee ſet downe) yee ſhall finde,
coming out of this kingdome, the firſt
king *Alphonſus* ; the 3. daughters of
his ſonne *Sancius* ; *Thereſa* Queen of
Leon ; *Mafalda* Queen of *Caſtile*, after *Religionſe* of *S. Bernards* order :
and *Sancia* of the ſame order : The
Prince

Prince Ferdinand sonne to king Ihon the first, *and the Infanta Ioane daughter to king Alphonsus the fifth*, *all eminent for holynefs of life and miracles: wher, in many thoufand families again you shall not finde one.*

All thees Saintes, to the number of 24. haue fprong out of thees ten Catholick families within the fpace of about 400. yeares. And had vve looked further back to theyr firft beginning or theyr converfion to the Chriftian faith, everie familie would haue yealded more: for in Hungarie vve should yet haue found S. Stephan, and Emeric kings, and Ladiflaus Prince of that Kingdome. In Bohemia, S. VVenceflaus Martyr. In Auftria, S. Leopoldus. In Brabant, SS. Pipin, Arnulphus, Emebert, Begga, Gertrude, Gudula, Pharaildis, Reynaldis, VValtrudis, Aldegund, &c. and fo in the reft.

And to returne again to S. Elifabeth Queen of Portugall, Note, that of
her

her are come, 7. Emperours, confequently one after another : fix Empreffes: 36. Kings: and 43. Queenes.

All vvhich together is to bee feen as cleer as the funn ; in a table which I haue fett forth; to the honour of the fame Saint: and vvithall, that the devout reader may fee therin hovv men in this vvorlde (if they vvill cooperate with Gods preventing grace) notvvithftanding maieftie, greatnefs, might, honour, aud kingdome, may attaine to great holynefs: And that alfo beholding and confidering fo manie Saints, the Chriftian Princes that glorie to bee of theyr race may be therby fpurred and pricked on to virtue, and follovve theyr holyneff, and choofe them for Patrones, Aduocates, and guides, in the vnknowne vvay, of this life, and after in the iuft iudgement of the vpright iudge.

Thofe that haue the carde which I fet out, muft note, firft that it vvas not poffible to giue all the Queenes
place

place therin, or to set downe theyr names, because the piece is little, and also because many of them were maried to kings, whom it was no need to bring in: and those that are set downe are without crownes, excepting the Saints, and those that were heyres to kingdomes or princedomes, who by theyr mariages transferred them to other families.

Secondly, heer in is cleerly to bee seen, the right and lawfull succession of the kingdoms of Hungarie, and Bohemia, and all the Prouinces, and Dominions of the howse of Austria vnto the person of Ferdinando Emperour of the Romanes. Also the inheritance and succession not only of all the kingdomes of Spaine but also of Sicilie, and Naples, of the Dukedome of Burgundie, Brabant, and the rest of the Dominions of the lowe countries, lawfully to pertein and fall vpon the person of the Catholick king Philip the 4. Dominic Victor, and that not by force of armes, much less by prudence
and

and humane induſtrie: but only by the
diſpoſition and prouidēce of God: who
(Eccl.cap.10.) tranſlateth kingdomes
from nation to nation. VVhence may
bee ſeen the idleneſſ, and vanitie or
manifeſt impietie of ſuch as preferr
the inventions of theyr owne braines,
or, to ſpeak more properly, certaine
lawes of ſtate, before the prouidence
and care that God hath of the gouernement of Empires and Dominions:
and for theyr better ſafeguard and ſe-
curitie, ſett faith and conſcience à
ſide, offend God and his holy church.

Thirdly, all Potentates ſhall heer
note, that the ſtrongeſt caſtle, the chie-
feſt fortification and defence of theyr
eſtates is, ſincere faith, and Religion
not affected: for although the riches
and regions bee moued together, although the earth be in vprore, and
hell come in for à part: nothing of all
this can ſhake the Monarch that fea-
reth God, and loveth his church, and
doth not communicate nor participate
with the aduerſaries ther of, and is
zealous

zealous of sincere and perfect iustice.

Fourthly that no man may haue anie thing to say, if it seem to him that I haue done more then the decrees of the church do permit, touching the description of the 24. Saints. Because they bee not all in the Catalogue of the Canonised by order of the Romane church, althoug the greatest part of them bee so: yet the others shined and do as yet shine with many miracles in theyr seuerall places and prouinces: VVher they are holden, esteemed and reuerenced, for Saints; and of some of them the Martyrologes of theyr orders do make mention, so that no doubt being made of theyr sanctitie it remayneth that we endeauour to followe them. Ther is in the table à distinction, for the Saints Canonised, or Beatified, are in ouall circles with beames of glorie about theyr heads, the other in round circles without beames. And because the beatification of B. Ioane Queen of

Fran-

France, is laboured for at *Rome*, and
the decree from day to day expected,
shee is sett in an ouall circle.

For the rest, what thing soever
can bee desired more in the description of the carde : the markes and di-
stinctions therin sett downe, and
chiefly the branches of it doe shewe it
cleerly. Lett, this suffice, gentle
Reader, for thy direction ; enioy my
little labour, and take it thanckfully.

F. F. P.

Concordat cum origina-
li Teutonico Ita testor
5. Octobris 1628.

Fr. Franciscus Bel.

Imprimatur,

Fr. Franciscus à sancta Cla-
ra, Lector Theologiæ: Collegij S.
Bonauenturæ Duaci, Guardia-
nus, & R.P. Ministri Prouinciæ
Angliæ, Cis mare vices gerens.

A

SHORT DECLARATION
OF THE LIFE, VIR
TVES, AND MIRACLES OF

S. ELIZABETH,
CALLED THE
PEACE-MAKER:
QVEEN
OF
PORTVGALL.

───────────────

Of her parents and bringing vp.

THE FIRST CHAPTER.

THIS B. Sainte Elizabeth was daughter to Peeter king of Aragon, her mother was named Cõstancia, daughter of Manfredus, King of Cecilie and Cozen to the Emperour.

Frede-

Frederick, the second: Shee was borne in the yeare of our Lord 1272. In the reign of her grandfather james (of whose merits and good workes it is found vvritten that he builded and endowed, to the honor of the glorious mother of god, 2000.) churches when this happy child vvas Chriftned, they named her Elizabeth in memory of that other S. Elizabeth, daughter to Andrevv king of Hungary, vvho dyed before, in great holynes of life. and vvas numbred amongft the Saints by Gregory the 9. vvhofe fifter Called Violence, vvas wife to the forenamed james: and grandmother to this holy Saint. hir birthe did fo much reioyce her grandfather, that he presētly made peace with his fonne, her father; with whom he had bene long at variance; but novv at this ioyfull

time of her natiuity he cocluded
peace, between them, and tooke
this vvelcome guifte, his grand-
child home to his pallace, and
brought her vp vvith great care.
inftructing her in all vertues.
vvhen she vvas 6. yeares ould
her grandfather dyed, and she
vvas brought home to her fathers houfe, where in her tender
yeares she gaue great teftimo-
ny of her future vertues; by her
grauity and deuotion vvhich was
of great edification, for shee kepte the fame maner of Rule in all
her actions. and efpetially in her
praiers and deuotions which she
had learned of her grandfather,
and vvhen she vvas Come to the
age of 8. yeares she daily read the
7. hovvres of the diuine office :
vvith great deuotion and diligence, she vvas louing and charitable to the poore, giuing according

cording to her age all that she
could procure, at vvhich her father did very much admire afcri-
bing all the good fucces of his affaires to his daughters merits for
vvhich he gaue daily thankes
vnto almighty God.

Of the mariage of B. Saint Elizabeth.

THE II. CHAPTER.

THe fame of this holy Saint,
and her naturall indowments
vvher-vvith she vvas adorned
vvas fpred through the vvholl
vvorld fo that she vvas defired in
mariage by many Princes, to witt,
the Prince, of Naples, and the
Prince of Brittany who fent their
Embaffadores, to the king of A-
ragon her father to defire this
royall daughter in mariage, but
this vvas vnwelcome nevves, vn

to

to him vvho greaued to thinke
that he should part vvith his beloued daughter, and much more
grieuous vvas it to the holy Elizabeth, that fought after the heauenly Bridegroome not defiring
any earthly Prince. About this
time dyed Alphonfus, the 3. king
of Portugal, and after him reigned in his kingdome his fonne
Dionifius, vvho being novv fet-
led in his kingdome did Choofe
out 3. of the greateft Peeres,
of his Royalme, vvhom he fent
in Embaffage to the king of Aragon, to defire this his daughter
in mariage: the king at that time
kepte his Courte at Barcinona
where the aforfayde Embaffadores arriued, theyr names vveare
the Lord Iohn Velho, Lord
Iohn Martinium, and the Lord
Vafco Perez, vvho prefenting
their Embaffage to the king; he

deliberating vvith him felfe on
vvhich of thefe 3. Princes , he
should beftovve his daughter, fo
deare and delightfull vnto him,
in regard of her virtuous difpofition, at the laft he made choice
of the king of Portugall , rather
then either of the other tvvo
Princes, in regard they were not
as yet eftablished in theire kingdoms as the kinge Dionyfius was.
Befides, this king was not fo neer
in blood vnto the lady Elizabeth as the other tvvo Princes
vvere , all vvhich vvere Motiues
that made the king her father
vvilling to beftowe her vpon the
aforfayd king Dionyfius ; and fo
foone as confent was giuen ther-
vnto ; the Lord Velho as cheefe
of thefe Embaffadores, toke this
holy Elizabeth to vvife , in the
name of his king , vvho vnder-
ftanding therof did much reioyce
vvith

vvith all his fubiects , exceedingly congratulating this hopefull mariage, and vvith great defire expected her Coming:efteeming her as giuen them from heauen, vvhen shee vvas to depart from her fathers pallace, tovvards her husbands courte : the king her father vvith greate attendance. accompanied her to the borders of Caftile : vvhere shee vvas honorably receiued by Aminitius Sancius vvho at that time being hindred vvith vvarres. Gaue her to the protection , of his brother james: and the beft of the nobility of Caftile. At Brigante vpon the Borders of Portugall Alphonfus brother to the aforfaide king Dionyfius, avvaited her, and brought with him many Bishops and nobles of the land , honorably conducting her Royall parfon to Trancofie , vvhere the

kin₂

king did attend the Comming of
his bryde , and the mariage vvas
solemnised with vnspeakable ioy
of all. In the yeare of our lord
1282. the king gaue her for vvelcome (after the custome of Portugall)great speciall rents out of
certain citties, and also courtiers
and attendants, as beseemed her.

Of her holy life in her mariage state.

THE III. CHAPTER.

THis nevve state of life : and
great honor did not any
vvayes diminish her accustomed
deuotions: for although this holy
Queene vvere but 12. yeares of
age: yet did she measure and dis-
pose of all her affaires in due time
and knevve hovv to direct and
turne all her actions to the honour

nour of God ; as her mirthe into
modefty : her ioy into teares :
her ievvells and coftly apparell,
to sharpe difcipline and chafti-
fing her body . She vvas much
giuen to the feruice of God in
holy contemplation ; yet did she
neuer neglect her feruice and
due refpectes vnto the king her
husband : shee kepte a iuft ac-
counte hovv shee fpent the day:
rifing early in the morning to
read her Matines and Prime : and
fo foone as the Prieftes and mufi-
cians vvere ready to performe
the diuine feruice: she went with
fpeed to the Chappell vvhere she
heard mafs very deuoutly vpon
her knees : and after mafs hauing
reuerently kiffed the Priefts
hand she made her offering according to the folemnity of the
day : that she might not appeare
vvith empty hands before all-
mighty

mighty God, this being done she read the reſt of her hovvres : and this vvas her accuſtomed maner. all the time of her life:and for the laſt shee read the office of Our B. Lady. and the office of the dead: in the after noones shee vvent à gaine to the Chappell to heare the Veſperas , and to performe the reſt of her office : after which she gaue her ſelfe to holy contemplation vvherin she shed à boundance of teares that proceeded from the tendernes of her hart she alſo vſed to reade deuout bookes vvhich incite to virtue : and after this shee exerciſed her ſelfe in skilfull needle vvorke ; Chiefly to shun idleneſs and to giue others good example , she made vvith her ovvne handes all thinges that vvere neceſſary for the church , she vvent often to confeſſion and received the moſt holy

holy Sacrament , of the Altar with greate deuotion.

Of her greate abstinence , and how her fasting was confirmed with à miracle.

THE IV. CHAPTER.

THis holy Queene vvas not only à louer of praire but also of great abstinence, accustoming her selfe to à very spare diett:that her soule might be the more plea-asing vnto God : and besides the fasting days appointed by the holy church,she kepte 3. in à weeke and she likewise fasted the aduēt of our lord : and from the Eue of S. Iohn Baptist vntill the day of our B. ladyes assumption, and so-me times she fasted the lent of S. Michael when these fastes see-med easie to her,then did she fast the

the Freedayes and Saturdayes,
with the Eues of our lady and all
the Apoftles , vvith bread and
vvater: and she vvould haue proceeded further in fafting but that
the king her husband ouer ruled
her. This vvife and virtuous
Queene knevv vvel that coftly
meales greate banquettes , and
fine apparell was often times the
nurce of many finnes:and it pleafed God to shevv by à miracle
hovv pleafing the fobriety and
abftinence of this his hand maide
was vnto him ; for being fick at
Alanquerti , she vvas appointed
by the Doctor to drinke vvyne
for the recouery of her ftrength,
but she for the loue of abftinence did refufe to drinke it ,
verely beleeuing it was not good
for her health. For not she alone:
but all the kinges and Queenes of Portugall vvere noe drin-
kers

kers of vvyne : fo that it pleafed
almighty God vvonderfully to
looke vpon her , for as her waigh-
ting vvoman brought her tvvice
à Cuppe of Could vvater to
drink it vvas both times miraculoufly turned in to good vvyne .

*Of her mildnes to the poore , likewife
confirmed with à miracle.*

THE V. CHAPTER.

THis holy Queene vvas all
vvayes found milde and very charitable tovvards the poore
being euer vvilling and redy
to helpe and comfort them in
all that poffibly she might , fo
that her liberality feemed to go
aboue her Eftate , she neuer let
any depart from her vncõforted
although there came many vnto
her , not fo much driuen by corporall

porall neceffity as to receiue of
her fome confolation and eafe of
their griefes by her pious counfell, and virtuous example. She
had great compaffion vpon all
ftrangers : and ontlandishe pilgrims tenderly receiving and
charitably releeuing them according to their neceffity vvith
mony, Cloathes, and lodging.
She gaue to all Cloifters as vvell
of men as of vvomen, to the vt-
termoft of her povver. She did
much commiferate the difftref-
fed eftate of poore gentilmen
vvhich through any misfortune
vvere fallen to decay : and she
fought out meanes, to helpe
them. Likewife this pious Queene did vnderftand that vvithin
her Royalme vvere very many
vvomen of good account which
fuffered greate mifery for vvant
of maintenance. and therby vve-

re

re in danger to fall in to finne :
but she employed her moft truft𝔦
feruants to releeue theyre neceffity and by her meanes preferred
many in mariage : and although
her piety vvere alvvayes plenti-
fully manifefted to the needy ,
yet vpon fafting dayes : and in
the holy vveeke she exercifed
moft charity : and aparelling her
felfe in very poore Cloathes she
vvas prefent at all the ceremoni-
es of the holy Catholike church.
Vpon good frjday she washed the
feete of 13. poore men and hauing
done she humbly kiffed theyr
feete and gaue them nevve Cloathes . the like she did on holy
thursday to 13. poore vvomen.
It chanched that one of thefe
poore vvomen had à very foare
foot which was grieuously eaten
vvith à cancre: and being loath
the princefs should perceiue it
she

she drevve it backe, and gaue
her other foot to vvash, but the
holy Queene tooke the foare
foot into her hand and vvashed
it very tenderly and although it
had fo ftrong à fauour that it
could hardly be endured yet did
she humbly kifs it, vvherupon
the faide foare vvas imediatly
healed miraculoufly. The like
pious worke she did vpon à good
friday at Scalabi, vvhen all the
people vvere gone but only one
poore man who ftayd in the court
to feeke fome remedy ofà foare
difeafe vvith vvhich he vvas afflicted, the porter feeing him was
very angry and in à great fury
required of him hovv he came to
be infected vvith fuch à grieuous
difeafe, and vvhy he did not goe
avvay with the other people and
taking à ftaff in his hand did beat
this poore man and vvound him
                              very

very grieuoufly. this vvicked
deed vvas made knovven vnto
the holy Queene, vvho did grieue very much at that her feiuant
had done, and caufed the poore
man to be brought vnto her and
comforted him in all that she
could, binding vp his vvoundes
vvith her owne handes and gaue
order to her feruants that they-
should haue care of him : but it
pleafed God that the next day ,
he vvas cured , and came to the
holy Queen to giue her thankes
for his health. she continued her
acuftomed charity and liberaly-
tie to the poore vvhich vvas she-
vved to be moft pleafing to the
diuine bounty by this vvhich follovveth. It chanced on à time as
she carried in her lapp à greate
fumme of mony to giue to the
poore, she mett vvith the king
her husband who fayed vnto her,
 C vvhat

what is that my beloued that you
carry there? she anſvvered they
be roſes: and opening her lapp
the mony vvas miraculouſly turned in to fayre roſes vvhich did
yeeld forth à very fragrant ſmel-
le: although it vvere then the time of vvinter; and hereof it co-
meth that this holy Elizabeth, is
alvvayes painted houlding roſes
in her lapp: she vvas euer very
hard and ſparing to her ſelfe but
to the poore moſt milde and liberall.

*Of à certaine peace vvhich
she made.*

THE VI. CHAPTER.

With great right is this holy Queen ſtiled Pacifica,
which is as much to ſay as Peace-
maker for she ſeemeth to haue
been

been borne for that end, to make peace. There vvas à very dangerous accident hapned betvveen the king her husband and his brother Alphonfus about certain rentes and revenues, which were in queftion betvveene them: and the matter was growen vnto that pafs that it feemed impoffible, to be ended vvithout the sheding of much blood: but this vertuous Queene made peace betvveen them vvith her ovvne lofs: prefenting to them as à guift to make the peace à towne Called Cintram, and other tovvns of Portugall, vvith all her richeft reuenues. She knevve the office of à Queene vvas to appeafe the angry mind of the king and make peace betvvene him and his fubiectes ; alfo to admonish thofe in office to difcouer the deceipts of the enimies in the court : She

coun-

counfelled the king to be alwayes liberall to thofe that deferued well : and not to giue eare to
thofe that backbite and detract
others : and when she knevve of
any that were at debate then did
she labour all that shee might to
pacifie them, making conditions
that theymight not go to lavve
and if the partyes vvere poore
that fuftained the iniury she
gaue them of her ovvne goods
becaufe the peace should not be
broken : yet vvithout detriment
to iuftice if there were any thing
that deferued punishment. This
holy Queen likewife made peace
betvveen the king of Aragon
her brother, and her daughters
husband Ferdinandus king of
Caftile : vvhich although many
Prieftes, and Bishops had vnder-
taken and could not bring to
pafs , yet she by her indeuours
                              brought

brought it to ſo good an end that they both did chooſe the king her husband to decide the matter : and at an other time this pious Queene made peace betvveen her ſonn in lavve Ferdinandus king of Caſtile , and her husband the king , that vvere both vp in armes and ready to giue battell; and vvhen the Prince Alphonſus had rebelled 2. or 3. times, and had taken in, one of his citties she ſo ouer came him vvith faire vvords and iuſt reaſons that she brought him home again to the ſeruice of his father: and therby quieted the Ciuill vvarres in Portugall.

C 3   *of*

Of her patience in tribulation.

THE VII. CHAPTER.

ALthough this holy Queene
had alvvayes her defires and
endeauors exercifed in the making of peace : and feeking to
conferue it, yet could she not her
felfe be exempted from enuious
tongues : for, there vvere fome
that fought to raife à great flan-
der of her and to fet debate betvveene her and the king her
husband, perfvvading him that
the Queene did giue intelligence
to her fonne Alphonfus of all his
fathers decrees, and that vvas the
reafon that the kings Army had
alvvayes fuch ill fuccefs, and fo
often ouerthrovve and his fonn
Alphonfo the victory. The king
being thus incenfed à gainft his
virtuous

virtuous and moſt innocēt queene: became ſo enraged vvith her
that he depriued her of all her
rentes and reuenues , and in ba-
niſhment ſent her to Alanquer
giuing her that place for her pri-
ſon : and this cauſed great grief
to all the Royalme but eſpecially
to the gouernours of her Caſtel-
les, vvho all promiſed to defend
her innocencie and right her
vvronges vvith theyr ſvvordes :
but ſhe refuſed all human helpe and putting her truſt only in
God, gaue her ſelfe wholly to her
deuotions ſpending the dayes
and nights in holy praier chaſti-
ſing her body vvith very ſore penance: all the vveeke long eating
or drinking nothing but dry
bread and could vvater ; and
vvhen the kinge her husband vnderſtood of her great auſterity,
and vertuous maner of liuing he

vvas moued to pitty: and it pleafed Almighty God to open his
eyes fo that beleeuing her innocencie he caufed her to be
brought home againe according
to her Princely eftate, and after
vvard she vvas held in greater
eftimation.

*Of her loue and loyalty to the king
her husband.*

THE VIII. CHAPTER.

THe vvifdome and conftan-
cie of this holy Queene hath
shined in all the courfe of her
life , but efpetially it vvas made
manifeft by the great patience
vvhervvith she did beare the dif-
loyall and difordered life of her
husband , and his loue to other
vvomen , by vvhom he had children : forgetting his plyted faith
vnto

vnto his vertuous Queene , and
louing vvife, vvho grieued very
much for two caufes,theone, that
Almighty God was fo much of-
fended , and the other, that the
fubieċts through the kings euill
example might be incited to follovv his leud life. The children
vvhich he had by other vvomen
she did not hate like à ftep mother , but brought them vp with
tender care , and motherly loue,
inftruċting them in all virtue as
if they had bene her ovvne , at
vvhich the king did very much
vvonder, and therby was moued
to amend his life and not any
more to wrong his mariage eftate, yet ther vvere ftill malitious
mindes vvhich fought to auert
his loue from this his virtuous
Queene: by raifing à newe flan-
der againft her innocencie,it was
in this maner. Ther vvas à yong
cour-

courtier , that bare great hatred
vnto another courtier of good
and orderly life , and one vvhom
this vertuous Queene did much
employ to carry almes to poore
folkes , and such like seruice , it
came to pass that the enuious
yong man taking in à vvrong
sence the charitable endeavors of
this pious Queene , did accuse
her to be disloyall to the king her
husband with this yong man: the
king being thus incensed sought
by all meanes to put the yong
man to death : and there vpon
cōmanded secretly the men that
kepte his lime kelles, to take the
first man he should send to them,
and bind him and cast him in to
the burning fornace. So the king
sent the innocent yong man to
be burnt , vvho vvent, not mis-
trusting any such matter, and as
he was going on the way he heard
the

the bell ring to the eleuation of
the B. Sacrament in the mafs: and
according to the cuftome vvent
in to the church to pray, as he had
bene vvarned by his father to do
at fuch times , and being there
vvere more maffes to be faid, he
ftayed ftill to keepe his deuotion.
The king defirous to heare of his
death , fent the falfe accufer to
the men of the lime kelle , to
knowe if they had performed his
command ; they taking him for
the man they should deftroy ,
anfvvered that they had not yet,
but novv they would, and fo they
tooke him prefently and caft him
headlong into the burning fornace. vvhen the nevves vvas
brought to the king by the firft
meffager , he ftoode amazed at
this vvonderfull and righteous
vvorke of God feeing evill coun-
fel alwaies to fall heavieft vpon
the

the counseller, and that the innocent Queen vvas thus preserued
from the slander.

Of her children.

THE IX. CHAPTER.

IT pleased God that her first
child vvas à daughter, vvhom
she named Constancia, after her
grand-mother, this daughter was
after vvard maried to Ferdinandus the 3. of that name, king of
Castile, vvith great ioye, but it
vvas soone turned into sorrovve
by the nevves of her sodain and
vnexpected death : for as this
Queene Elizabeth with the king
her husband vvent from Scalabi to Arambuiam , ther came
an hermite in great sorrovv ,
and desired to speake vvith the
Queene : she gaue him audience,

ce, vvho fayed vnto her. I shall
declare vnto your highnefs moft
fad and heavie nevves ; your
daughter is fodainly departed
this life, and her forrowfull foule
hath appeared openly to me in
my chappell and prayed me to
giue you to vnderftand that she
is in purgatory, and she defired the holy facrifice of the mafs
might be offered a vvholl year
for her releafe. The pious mother
fulfilled the defire of her daughter: and the yeare being accom-
plished her daughter appeared to
her in Conymbria in her fleep,
clothed in white, and feeming
to be full of ioy, called her mother by her name faying, mother
Elizabeth almighty God vvill re-
vvard you in heauen, vvhither
novv I goe releafed from all paine. Heervpon the Queen vva-
ked and fmiling vvith ioy vvent
                              prefent-

prefently to the paftor and vnderftood by him that her daughters apparition vvas vpon the
maffes concluding : at vvhich
she vvas much comforted. The
17. year of her age she bare her
daughter Conftancia and the 20.
year of her age she bare her fonne Alphonfus, at Conimbria, and
he reigned after the death of his
father.

Of her pious workes shewed in the
building of many holy places.

THE X. CHAPTER.

THis holy Queene vvas very
milde , and benigne to all
fortes of people, but efpetially
shee had regard vnto the commun good and publike profit ,
for vvhen she vnderftood of any
decayed churches or hofpitalles
shee

she prefently tooke order to
haue them repaired at her ovvne
coft and charges. Her piety in
this kind vvas fo greate, that à
Gentilvvoman dvvelling at Al-
mofterium not farr from Scalabi
began to build à cloyfter for
Nunnes of S. Bernards order: and
being preuentéd by death could
not make an end of it, but left
her begun vvorke to this holy
Elizabeth, who did moft willingly vndertake to finish it, to performe the laft will and teftament
of the deceffed. hauing finished
this good worke she left it richly
prouided of rentes, leauing the
name and honor therof vnto her
vvho did firft begin the vvorke.
The like to, this she did alfo at
Scalabi, for the Bishop of that
cittie began an almes houfe for
found-linges but being preuen-
ted by death, could not finish it,
and

and in his laſt vvil he commen-
ded his vvork to the holy Queen
Elizabeth , much deſiring that
she vvould not by any meanes
leaue it vndone: the Queene did
not only accomplish his deſire
in this, but alſo made the vvork
much greater and augmented
the rents , and gaue good order for the gouernment of the
houſe, her ſelfe did giue the children to eate , out of motherly
loue , and vvhen they vvere
grovvne bigg she put them to
learne ſuch trades as they vvere
found capable of. This holy
Queenes virtue vvas ſeen in the
vvillingnes vvhervvith she vn-
dertooke to finish vvorkes begun by others, vvherin she knew
there was more labour and charges for her then any applauſe of
the vvorld: for she ſought nothing but the honor of God in
all

all her actions, and the faluation
of foules, and commun vvealths
good. There vvas à Cloifter of S.
Clares order in Conimbria very
little both church and houfe, in
regard it was begun by à Gentilvvoman that could not finish it
for vvant of meanes: and this holy Elizabeth bought houfes and
grovvnd ioyning to the Cloifter,
to inlarge it. she made an hofpi-
tal by her pallace: vvherin she
maintained 15. poore men, and
as many poore women, she builded alfo à houfe in the Citty of
Nouarium for vvomen that having proftituted theyr honeftie,
were converted from theyr lewd
life to good.

D   of

Of the death and buriall of her huſ-
band and how she liued after
his death.

THE XI. CHAPTER.

THe loue and loyalty this holy Queene bare to her huſ-
band vvas moſt eſpetially mani-
feſted in his ſicknes , in and after
his death, for firſt she offered many prayers and good vvorkes for
his conuerſion , humbly implo-
ring the diuine mercy for him ,
and ſeeking by all meanes to
purge his ſoule from ſinn , that
he might vvithout ſpot depart
this life : for that effect she gaue
very much almes,with deſire that
his life might be prolonged if it
vvere the diuine vvill . But it
pleaſed God ſo to diſpoſe that the
king , her husband dyed at that
time:

time : and although she were left
in greate forow yet she made not
much shew exteriourly,but layed
avvay her Coftly apparell and in
the middeft of her grief thought
more vpon her foules health then
any fpeaches of men : and in this
pious confideration she tooke
the habit of the poore Clares:and
cutting of her haire and girding
her felfe vvith à cord, attired in
this holy habit,in humble maner
she appeared before the peeres
and nobles of the land,who ftood
all round about the corps , and
she fayed vnto them vvith à fad
and forovvfull voyce, thinke my
good lords , that the Queene is
alfo dead vvith the king : and
let it be your care to bury him
with kingly armes as becometh à
king : but for my felfe j haue no
need of any Courtly attendance,
as ladyes of honor , or any other

ſeruants : neither let this attire
you ſee me vveare ſeeme ſtrange
vnto you , for this shal be the laſt
act of mourning, this habit shall
bring vnto my memory the
death of my deceſſed husband :
my head shorn and couered with
this holy veile shall vvitneſs the
fidelity of Elizabeth: this vnwon-
ted ſpectacle shall incite all to
lament ; and hauing ended this
ſpeach which cauſed much grieff
to all that vvere preſent she
ſpake many comfortable vvor-
des to the nobility, giuing ſuch
vviſe and prudent reaſons for
what she did, that they remained
both ſatisfied and edified. This
holy Queene was preſent to ſee
her husbands funerall ſolemni-
zed vvith great honor , and her
ſonne Alphonſus , vvith many
Prelates and Princes follovved
the corps loaden vvith ſorrovv :

after

after them follovved the holy Elizabeth to the wonder of all beholders : in this fort they vvent till they came to à Cloifter of Nunnes of S. Bernards order : vvhich the king before had builded not far from the Citty , ther he had defired to be buried , and according to his defire it was done. The funeral being ended, and all returned home, the Queene ftayed by the toombe , not fo much to bevvaile her vvidovv-hood , as to help the foule of her husband vvith praiers and good vvorkes, for there was no naked, or needy poore , but she clothed and releeued: the maffes she caufed to be fayed for him vvere innumerable. thefe thinges done, she vvent to Conimbria, becaufe she vvold not giue her Nobles too much forrovv by parting from them quite. She had à pri-

D 3   vate

vate way from her pallace to the
Cloifter of the poore Clares, with
vvhom she conuerfed much, but
fo as not to bind her felfe to them:
yet she vvent to the quire vvith
the religious to performe the diuine office , and did exercife her
felfe in all humble workes vvith
them according as time gaue her
leaue. She vifited other Cloifters, churches, and holy places,
not only thofe that vvere neer
hand , but alfo fuch as vvere farr
off, giuing her offering vvith her
ovvne hand : and that she might
the better attend to the help and
reliefe of poore people , she was
counfelled to take vpon her the
third Rule of S. Francis vvhich
she did, and kept it alwayes after,
to the end of her life.

Hovv

How S. Elisabeth went to Galicia to vi-
sit S. Iames in Compostella and
of the offering she made.

THE XII. CHAPTER.

NOt fully à yeare after the
death of the king her husband, this holy Queene tooke
her vvay towardes Compostella,
vvith all her court, to visit the
body of the holy Apostell S. Iames, but none knew whither she
intended to go till she had travailed some dayes iourny, and
passed the rivers of Dure and Mi-
nie, then they all imagined by
her deuout and holy maner of
life vvhither she vvent. When
they came neer to the Citty, so
that they could see the tops of
the steeples, the Queene aligh-
ted and vvent thither on foott,

D 4 to

to the vvonder of all her follow-
ers. It is not poffible to declare
vvith vvhat great deuotion and
reuerence she honored the body
of the Apoftel, and ftayed ther
vntill the day of his feaft, atten-
ding vvith more then ordinary
deuotion at the folemnity therof
till all vvas finished : she like-
vvife gaue to vnderftand vvith
vvhat affection she vvare her
coftly attire whileft her husband
liued : for at that time she beftovved all her beft apparel imbro-
dered with pretious ftones vpon
that holy place: she gaue alfo her
Royall Crowne : vvith her gould
and filuer plate to adorn the
temple. She gaue moreover à
faire mule, with à gould bridell,
with the armes of Portugall, and
Aragon : and à great fum of mony, vvith other coftly guifts,
vvhich she beftovved on that
pla-

place , in honor of the glorious
Apoftle S. Iames : vvhere they
are feene to the great admira-
tion of all people vvho neuer
beheld fuch riches . Hauing finished her deuotion the Archbishop gaue her à mantell and
à ftaff that she might be like to
other Pilgrims.

How shee builded the Cloifter of S.
Clare , after her returne
to the Kingdome.

THE XIII. CHAPTER.

BEeing novv returned home,
shee kept the folemnity of
the yeare day , of her deceafed
husband , at Odiuille vvith Al-
ponfus her Sonne, and many Bif-
hops and great nobles, which folemnity beeing finished, shee returned to Conimbria , to finish à
Cloi-

Cloyſter of S. Clare vvhich ſhee
had begun , vvhere-vnto ſhee
gaue her gold chaynes and other
rich attire. ſhee cauſed tobe ſent
for , all ſuch tradeſmen as make
things neceſſary for the ſeruice
of the church, as chalices, croſſes,
tabernacles, candleſtickes, lamps
and all other maner of church
ſtuff vvhat ſoeuer, vſed in the ſeruice of God : one part ſhee gaue
to the Cloyſter , an other part
to other churches in Portugal.
Some ritch and coſtly guifts and
ievvels ſhee gaue vnto her maried daughter, ſome to her coſen,
ſome alſo vnto Queene Mary of
Caſtile , and ſome to Leonora
Queene of Aragon and other
Princeſſes vvho vvere neer vnto
her in blood , from thence forth
to liue in ſimplicity and pouerty
vvith great ſtrictnes, to finiſh the
reſt of her life. This holy Princeſs

cefs with great care and diligēce
finished the Cloifter of S. Clare
vvith the church, before mentioned (for to that end shee came
to Conimbria) and made for her
felfe à houfe adioyning to the
Cloyfter, that from thence shee
might come to the fifters, to forvvard the vvorkemen, shee like-
vvife encreafed the rents of the
fame Cloifter, and the number
of fifters. In building shee had
great vnder-ftanding. In the
church of the aforfaide Cloifter
shee caufed to be made for her à
tombe wherein at her death shee
intended to be buried. In the
building of the tombe there being à great ftone which theworck
men could not remoue out of
the place, the holy Queene
laying her hand vpon the ftone
it vvas very eafily after vvardes
remoued to the right place, without

out labour, vvhich could not bee
but by miracle.

*Hovv the riuer Tagus vvas parted to
make vvay for the holy Queene,
and of one blinde, vvhom
shee cured.*

THE XIV. CHAPTER.

HEere alfo follovveth à vvorthy miracle, that God did
vnto this holy Queene, in the
Kingly river Tagus, vvhich runneth by the Cittie of Scalabi.
Ther is in this vvater made by
handes of Angells the fepulcher
of S. Irene, after the maner of S.
Clements: this holy Queene had à
very great defire to vifit the faide
Sepulcher but feeing shee could
not pafs vnto it, through the water, shee prayed on the banck
vvith bended knees, and eyes
full

full of teares, vvhen behold, the
vvater parted it felf the Sepulcher apeared, and she vvith great
deuotion vvent betvvixt the wa-
ters vpon the fandes,giuing thankes to God, and to the holy S.for
fo great grace and fauor. Ther,
vvith great reuerence beholding
the B. Body, novv and then kif-
fing it deuoutly, shee continued
in prayer all the vvhole day. At
her retorne, the forfaid vvater
follovved her with fo foft à pafe
as though it had bene à feruant
to attend her, vntill shee vvas
paffed ouer. Befides this miracle,
I shall declare another; this virtuous Queene deliuered many
people from diuers very gree-
uous infirmities, and great dan-
gers, but one maide borne blind
she cured by only touching her
eyes, vvith her holy hand.

Of her

Of her sobrietie in her widowhood,
and the profitable spending of
her time.

THE XV. CHAPTER.

WEe haue declared hovv so-
ber, and abſtinent this holy Queene vvas vvhen her huf-
band liued, and hovv she obſer-
ued many faſting dayes. This
virtue shee did not only practiſe
in her yonger yeares, but alſo
grovvne ould shee vvas very
ſtrict in faſting. While her huf-
band lived, shee could not faſt ſoe
much as shee did deſier, beeing
hee had forbid her, but after the
death of the king, her faſts were
both long and many, follovving
her owne deuotion ſo much, as
shee vvould not only abſtein
from coſtly, and delicate dyet,
but

but alſo from ſuffiſing her nature
with poore and ordinary meates,
notvvithſtanding that shee vvas
very necre 60.yeares of age. The
pious Princeſs knevv right vvell
hovv to deuide the time both of
night and day to her ovvne profit. Shee had allvvayes vvith her
5. Siſters of the poore Clares:
shee roſe in the night to reade
her mattins vvith them, in her
Chappel, they alſo read Primo
together, and after heard Maſs,
vvith great recollection, then
she gaue her ſelfe vvholy to meditation, vpon the paſſion of our
lord Ieſus, vvith very tender affection sheeding forth aboundance of teares, both for her
ovvne ſiñes, and others, and
praying for the ſaluation of all.
The priuate maſs being ended,
shee hearde ſolemne maſs for the
ſoule of her husband, after that
she

she heard another priuate mafs,
fo that shee let no day pafs without hearing of 3. maffes vvhich
being done shee toke fome neceffary refe&ion for the ftreng-
thning of her body, though with
greater defire shee thirfted after
heauély foode. After dinner shee
caufed the vvorkemen to be called, and hearing theyr reconning
gaue order for building of what
remained to be finished. After
this she gaue audience to all, not
letting any depart difconfolate.
Then did shee retire in to her
chamber to recolle& her felfe:
and then she vvent to her chappell to heare the Vefperas, and
Complin: vvhich she alfo read in
à lower voyce with the religious.
Her deuotions being ended she
tooke her fupper, if it vvere not
fafting day, as vvith her it vvas
alvvayes for the moft part; and
after

after this she difposed her felfe
to take her reft. She vvas of very
little fleepe, rifing in the nights,
halfe Clothed, she prayed vpon
the bare grovvnd vvith fighes
and grones, vvith her eyes eleua-
ted tovvardes heauen, and then
caft down to the feet of crucified
Iefus she humbly implored the
higheft to take mercy vpon her,
and the foule of her husband.
Thus praying she vvould ftrike
her breft to refift fleepe till she
could no more. Her recreation
vvas, not in feing playes, nor
any other vaine delightes of this
world, but her greateft ioy vvas
to be vvith the Clariffes, vvhere
she often remained in her littell
houfe she had caufed to be builded by the port of the Cloifter,
that she might liue and take her
refection vvith them. She counfelled fpirituall perfons to labor

E   for

for the perfection of their estate,
and to be faithfull and loyall to
theyr heauenly spous, this vvas
the delight of holy Elizabeth:she
reioyced exceedingly vvhen any
yong virgins gaue them selues
to the seruice of God : as it appeared in the vvillingnes vvher
with she gaue leaue to her sisters
daughter vvho desired to be à
Clarifs , furthering her therin
after she had vvel tryed her constancy.

Of her humilitie and meeknes to all
sortes of people.

THE XVI. CHAPTER.

THis holy Saint Elizabeth did
manifest her loue and mildnes to all that vvere in any ne-
cessity , assisting them in all charity vvithout any exception of
par-

parſons.When she receiued iniury from any, she did not only
pardon the offenders, but would
not ſuffer them to be punished
for ought done vnto her ſelfe.
She did ſo vvillingly forgiue all
offences that she was neuer ſeene
to be angry at any time : follovving herein the example of S.
Elizabeth Queene of Hungarie,
after vvhom she vvas named, as
is à forſayed. She builded an hoſ-
pitall neere to her houſe, for the
releefe of poore people and di-
uided it into tvvo ſeuerall dwel-
lings the one for men, and the
other for vvomen, vvith all ne-
ceſſaryes for theyr vſe. She receiued in to it 15. poore people of either ſexe : admonishing
them to liue vvel and orderly,
and to haue patience in ſicknes
and pouerty : she ordained à
Chappell and à maſs to be ſayed

therin

therin euery day for theyr fpirituall comfort: and for theyr corporall she clothed them euery
yeare, and ferued them like à feruant, dreffing theyr meat and hel-
ping vvith great affection thofe
that vvere ficke, lifting them
vp, and laying theyr pillovves as
she thought vvould giue them
moft eafe. Ther was not any ficknes hovv dangerous fo euer that
could vvithdravv her from the
feruice of the poore. Her charity abounded in à time of great
neceffity, vvhen at Conimbria
ther vvas fo great à dearth, that
many dyed of hunger : for her
Pallace vvas à receptacle of the
poore vvhom she releeued vvith
corne, meat and mony, hauing
rather to dy her felfe, then liue
to fee others in vvant. She like-
vvife prouided for all Cloifters,
and tooke care to bury the dead.
Many

Many of the courtiers feared her
liberality vvould bring her and
them to fuffer miferie, and therfore they vfed to put her in mind
to take care of her ovvn family,
vvhervnto she vvas bound:theyr
folicitation in this kind much
greeued her, and she requefted
them not to feare for almighty
God vvould not permit them to
vvant.

Hovv the holy Elizabeth vvent difgui-
fed, to S. Iames, to
Compoftella.

THE XVII. CHAPTER.

HAuing finished the Cloifter
of S. Clare and reflecting
vpon the goodnes of God shewed
to her, and many other Princes
and kings vvhom shee had out-
lived : she defired very earneftly

to be

to be releafed of this life, and to
be vvith Iefus Chrift. Vnderftanding that at Compoftella ther
vvas à great Iubile, à poena &
culpa, fecretly vvithout knowledge of her courtiers, in
ftrange apparell, and à ftaff in
her hand, she vvent thither-
wardes 64. yeares ould all alone,
vnlefs vvith one or tvvo of her
Chamberlaines : not vvithftan-
ding that it vvas then the heat of
fummer. She caryed her Clothes
and other neceffary thinges on
her backe, begging like à poore
vvoman almes for Goddef-fake.
It hath not been often heard that
any Queene travailed in this maner. This pilgrimage she made
but one yeare before her death.
At her returne home she was en-
treated to make peace betvveen
her fonne Alphonfus, and her
daughters fonne king of Caftille,
                                  called

called alſo Alphonſus, but she
could not effect it, being preuen-
ted by death.

Of the death of this holy Queene.

THE XVIII. CHAPTER.

AS the holy Queen trauailed
towardes Eſtrimotium ther
to treat of the afore named peace
vvith her ſonne Alphonſus, it
pleaſed almighty God that she
fell in to infirmity which ſeemed
at firſt little, but aftervvard
great. Before her extremitie of
ſicknes she came euery day to
the Chappel to heare diuine ſeruice accompanied with the king
her ſonn, and hauing ſetteled all
her afaires with him and his wife,
her ſicknes increaſed ſo much
vpon à munday that she kept her

E 4   cham-

chamber, and the kings daughter, her grand child tended her
very carefully In this ficknes she
was vifited by the moft glorious
Virgin Mary vvho came accompanied vvith à great troupe of
Virgins all in vvhite vvith crownes of gould vpon theyr heades,
affectionatly bovving them felues tovvard her: vvhich the holy
Elizabeth feeing, and percei-
uing them to come neere vnto
her, she defired the Queene her
daughter in lavv, and the reft of
thofe who were prefent that they
vvould giue place to that heauenly company:then feeling her
death to aproache she fent for
her Confeffor, and hauing made
her confeffion she made him fay
mafs in another roome wher she
might both fee and heare it. The
mafs being ended, hauing alone
put on her Religious habit, she
                              forced

forced her felfe with great paine
to go to the Altar , vvhere she
receiued the moſt holy Sacrament deuoutly vpon her knees
the fame day that she rendred
her bleſſed foule in to the hands
of her creator Hauing ended her
deuotion at the altar , she returned to her bedd. About euening
(although the Doctors did not
think she vvould haue departed
ſo ſpeedily) she called for her
fonn and treated with him of the
peace for vvhich she had come
thither ; after this she deſired him
to go to ſupper , and as he vvas
going out vvith the Doctor , he
heard à ſodain crye of all that
were in the chãber , and coming
in, he called vpon his dying mother ; and kiſſing her hand she
came à little to her felfe and ſpake to him, about thinges of very
greate importance : and after ,
tur-

turning her felfe she caft her
eyes vpon à crucifix and calling
vpon our bleſſed lady vvhom she
had feen in her ficknes she gaue
her ſpirit into the hands of her
redeemer . Anno 1336. being
the 4. of Iuly : she vvas, 65. yeares of age vvhen she dyed.

Of her Buriall.

THE XIX. CHAPTER.

AS foone as the holy foule was
departed from the bodie ,
they opened her teftamēt: where
they found that shee had char-
ged her fonne Alphonfus to bu-
rie her bodie at Conimbria in the
church of S. Clare that she had
made. Heerto he appointed the
the principaleft of his court,who
much feared to carry the body fo
farr, by reafon of the heat of the

time: but the king would accomplish his mothers vvill. The bodie being shut in à coffin , and layde vpon à waggon·by the shaking vpon the vvay , some moisture issued through the chinckes of the chest: vvhich they perceiving that had the care of the body, began to murmur against the king , fearing the evill smel which they presumed would follovve. Heer vpon came one of them to the coffin and felt so svveet à sauour as hee sayde hee had never felt the like : the rest approaching felt the same : and all of them iudged it to bee an odour from heauen. On the seaventh day they arriued at Conimbria, vvhen all the cittie and kingdome was filled with sorrow for the death of so good à Queen. After solemne seruice, the bodie was layde in the graue which before

fore she had caufed to bee made:
and it chaunced that the handes
and cloathes of the men that
laydit in were befprinckled with
à liquor that came out of the bodie: vvhich gaue fuch à fweet favour as it exceeded the favour of
rofes or the fvveeteft flovvers.

*Of the miracles which happened after
her death.*

THE XX. CHAPTER.

AFter the death of this holy
Queen, many miracles were
vvrought, by vvhich her me-
rites before Almightie God
vvere made knovven to the
vvorlde.

Tvvo men that had long been
fick of violent agues caried the
Bear in which the holy body had
layen, and comending themfelues

felues to the merits of this Saint
Elizabeth vvere forthvvith cured.

A Clarifs had long time fo
great paine in her head and teeth
that shee could eat no meat: but
coming to theBear she was forth-
with cured.

Ferdinand Stephans à citizen
of Conimbria had his foote hurt
vvith à nayle vvhich by no meanes could be dravven out , and
commending himfelfe to this
holy Queen was prefently hol-
pen.

A vvoman that had the pefti-
lence, and à carbuncle vpon her
hand , winding it in à cloath that
the holy Elizabeth had vfed, was
prefently cured.

Tvvo blind vvomen vifiting
her graue received fight inftantly.

The mother of à Canon Regu-
lar

lar being blinde, and by her
sonne lead to the graue : hauing
the re done her deuotion, vvas
restored to cleer sight instantly.

Manie others of sundry disea-
ses, as of hoat agues, burning fe-
vers, possessed by the divell,
blind, distract of theyr vvittes,
&c. coming to her graue, or
being annoynted vvith the oyle
that burned in her lampe : vver
miraculously cured.

*Howe it came to paß that her feast was
kepte:and how her holy body was
found entire, and honora-
bly taken vp.*

THE XXI CHAPTER.

THe king Emanuell vnder-
standing of the miracles done by the merits of the holy S.E-
lisabeth, obtained of Pope Leo
the

the X. that in the diocefs of Conimbria her feaft day might bee
folemnized:and king Ihon the 3.
fonne of Alphonfus, obtained of
Pope Paul the IIII. that the fame
might be kept over all Portugall.
Almightie God by 3.wonderfull
miracles did shevv hovv pleafing
this folemnitie was vnto him:for
three Clariffes afflicted vvith incurable difeafes , were healed
therat: After this, Philip the 3.of
that name king of Spaine and
Portugall, procured that fix perfons of note should bee ordeined
to feeke out the miracles of this
holy Elifabeth,which being done
verie carefully , the forenamed
king fent to Rome to Pope Pau-
le the V. to the end she might bee
Canonifed : but the Pope dying
it vvas not then brought to pafs.
At laft the prefent Pope Vrbanus
the VIII. at the requeft of King
Philip

Philip the 4. made the forefayd
inquifition of the miracles,where
after 276. yeares that shee had
been dead, to vvitt, in the year of
our lorde 16 1 2. her graue hauing
been opened in prefence of many vvitneffes , and expert Doc-
tours of Phifick : they found in
the toombe à cheft of vvood covered with ox hides which began
to bee rotten, shut with barres of
yrō, that were eaten vp with ruft:
the bodie wound in duble filke :
the face honorably covered to
the breft with a cypres veile. The
bodie vvas all entire and vvhole,
the face vvith liuely colour as if
she had been but newly buried :
and the linen cloathes about her
ftill fo nevve , as vvithout great
ftreffthey could not bee torne.
A Religious man that was there,
called IhonDelgado touched the
face of the Queen vvhich received

ved the print of his fingers. The
great Doctor of Physick Baltha-
zar Azeredo drevv to him three
times her arme and it went backe
to the place everie time vvithout breaking. Ther vvas found
by her in the graue à staff and à
purse, vvhich betokened her virtuous life, and liberalitie to the
poore : vvith the staff she had
gone on pilgrimage to S. Iames.
Out of the purse shee had rea-
ched money to the needy. The
Bishop Alphonsus Albicastre, because this ritch treasure had been
found in his diocess, made (with
consent of the king) to the honour of the holy Elisabeth, à cost-
ly chappel of polished marble,
vvtih à guilded arch, vnder the
vvhich he placed à siluer shrine,
vvith vvindovves to bee opened
that as need vvas the body might
be seen, as vvel vvithout, of the

F   people

people : as vvithin of the Religious. This good Bishop after he
had beſtovved 12000. crovvnes
vpon the vvorck, being preuen-
ted by death could not finish it :
he left vvith the king of Spaine
30000. crovvnes for the Cano-
niſation , vvho himſelfe did for-
der it, but being taken avvay by
death ſavve it not done. in fine,
it was brought to an end by king
Philip the 4. and she is Canoni-
ſed by Pope Vrban the VIII. in
the year of Iubile 1625. the 25.
of May , to the honour and glorie of God.

FINIS.

An Abridgment of Christian Perfection (*STC* 11538.5) is reproduced, by permission, from the unique copy at the English College, Rome. The text block of the copy measures 100 × 51 mm.

In a departure from the rigorously unenhanced reproduction of the facsimiles in this series, slight enhancements of faint letters have very occasionally been made to the text reproduced below because this unique exemplar, missing for over half a century, is unavailable (and most likely will remain unavailable) to readers, except in this facsimile reproduction.

Pages 64, 65, 68 and 69 are mis-numbered.

XI A 22

2i

✠

An Abridgment
of Christian
Perfection.

✳

Auctore P. Achille Gagliardi
for his presse publ aning nomine
inpresny ed Baipiy se posten
kriverby Italice 1694
et Heng.

Collegij A N *Ongeare* *De wden*

A B R I D G M E N T

OF CHRISTIAN

P E R F E C T I O N.

Eubiardo *P Confoh any*

VVHEREIN

are conteyned many excellét Documents, Precepts, & Aduer-
tifments , touching the
holy, & facred myfticall
Diuinity..

*Tranflated out of the French corrected
Copie , into English.*

¶ Imprinted Anno M, D C, X I I.

MATTH. II.

Confiteor tibi Pater, Domine
cæli, & terræ : quia abscondi-
sti hæc à sapientibus, & pru-.
dentibus, & reuelasti ea par-
uulis.

TO THE
RELIGIOVS
OF OVR
NATION:
AND

To all such as desire to attayne to
the eminent estate of Chri-
stian Perfection, health
in our Lord.

THIS little worke conteineth and setteth before our eyes, doctrine of so great Perfection, and endeauoureth to purify the intention, in so high a degree, & to reduce the

mind of man to so great conformitie and vnion with the
will of God , that the view of
so great a light may be likely to
dazle the eyes of such as yet do
look through the clowd of self-
loue , ánd are not fully resol-
ued to resist , & repell their inward enemyes, and in that respect it is not intended or dire-
ctéd to any such : & much lesse
is it offered to sensuall minds ,
who cannot discerne the worth
of such a pearle , but would
rather trample it with their
feete , then tread the pathes
which lead to such a treasure .
But I doubt not to iudg it fitly
presented to the reading of all
such, as haue entred , or resol-
ued

ued to enter the pathes of Perfection, by imitation of Christ our Lord in practise and performance of the Counsells Euangelicall. For of such mindes we may with reason hope, that first God for his part, as he hath called them from the pursuite of worldly vanities to the veritie of his diuine loue : so he will be no lesse bountifull vnto them in assisting their endeauours with pléty of grace , vntill he haue perfected the worke which himselfe hath begun in their soules . And of their part, as they haue receaued from God so much light , as to find this treasure , and so much wisdome as to know the value

* 4 therof,

therof, and so much fortitude
of mind as to contemne their
former worldly estate, for the
purchase of this field or state
of religious life : so we may iu-
stly expect at their handes, that
according to the light , wise-
dome & fortitude, which they
haue receaued , they should be
desirous, and glad to labour in
getting out the said treasure,
and procuring it entirely into
their possession : and therfore
that they ought neither to be
loath to vndertake the labour
of digging , nor yet to thinke
much, hauing gottē the gould,
to seuer it frō the earth & drosſ
which adhereth vnto it . And
this true mind of benefiting
them-

themſelues (which is neuer
wanting in any wiſe man that
hath found but an earthly trea-
ſure) is as much as this booke
requireth , in the practiſe of
whatſoeuer is here preſcribed.

For firſt he is heere aduiſed
to dig & deſcend into his owne
nothing by *Anihilation* : then
to caſt vp and throw from him
all the earthy ſubſtance which
lieth betweene him & the trea-
ſure , and this by *Diſappropriation*, or as it is called in the Ghoſ-
pel, by *Renunciatiō* of all things
which he poſſeſſeth . Then is
he led by the vertue of *Indiffe-
rencie* to cleanſe it alſo being
found , from the duſt of his
priuate affections, and ſelf-in-
tereſt.

* 5

tereſt . And thus the gould
being gotten into his poſſeſſiõ
it then teacheth him firſt how
to purifie the ſame from the
droſſe of all ſelf-loue , by the
Conformitie of his will to the
will of God. Secondly to refine
it yet more from the baſer kind
of mettall , which is oftè much
mixed with this diuine gould,
and yet hardly by the eye to be
diſcerned : but the touchſtone
of Chriſt his example doth try
it, and the fire of Charitie doth
refine it , ſo that it then comes
to be *Aurum ignitum* , ſpoken
of in the Apocalyps , and one
thing, as it were, with the fire
it ſelfe ; and this is therfore
called *Vniformitie*. Then remaineth

neth only, that his gould thus feruent and pliable to the will of him that worketh it, receaue the stampe of the heauenly King, that so it may be currant coyne in his diuine Court: in which it is only a patient, and nothing is expected of it, but that it take without resistance what impression the workmã is best pleased to impose. This is the worke of grace in the soule, the workman is God himself, and the stampe he imprinteth in it, is his owne Image: and so this sixt & highest degree of perfection is called *Deiformitie*.

In this state the soule hauing first reiected all impediments

to her well-doing, rooted out
all euill habits, planted in her
self the habits of solid vertues,
and seuered from her intention
all self-loue: yea hauing by the
help of Gods grace, purified
euen her most inward desires,
and all sensible inclinations,
from the infection of self-in-
terest, then is her will not conformed only, but vnited vnto
the will of God, and so transformed into the same, that now
it seemeth not to be her will
that worketh, but the will of
God which worketh in her:
as though she had giuen her
owne hart vnto Christ: and,
as we read of *S. Catherine* of
Siena, had receaued his in ex-
change

change, to be in her from that
time forward, the beginning
and firſt motiue of all her operations.

Of which eſtate alſo we may
vnderſtand the wordes of the
Apoſtle *Gal.* 2. when he ſaid,
*Viuo autem, iam non ego, viuit
verò in me Chriſtus:* And I liue,
now not I, but Chriſt liueth
in me. Much like as we ſee the
ſienſe which is grafted into an
other ſtock, which liueth indeed in it ſelf, and bringeth
forth fruit, but not by the life
it had before, from it owne
naturall roote; but by the ſap
and life it now receaueth from
the new ſtock into which it is
inſerted, in which it groweth,
and

and by which it liueth.

To this moſt high and ex-
cellent Perfection this little
Treatiſe doth guide vs. To this
your deuout mindes, I aſſure
my ſelf, do aſpire. For the obtaining of this, I beſeech his diuine Goodnes to aſſiſt vs all
with his holy grace , and to
repleniſh your ſoules with the
comfort of his celeſtiall ſpirit , and to make me partaker
of your holy merits. This 27.
of Ianuarie 1612.

Yours in all Chriſtian dutie.

P. M.

TO THE
Reader.

IT is fit, gentle Reader, thou be aduertised that wheras both
in this Epistle, as al-
so in sundry partes
of this booke, there is mention
made, that when the will cōmeth
to be vnited, and as it were tranf-
formed into the will of God, that
then it muft be a patiēt rather thē
an agēt, according to which thou
fhalt alfo find many aduifes in the
booke,

booke (efpecially in the Chapters
of the fecôd & third eftate) where
he is taught that the foule muſl be
content to forgo firſt all aᶜtiue o-
peration and praᶜtice euen of vertues themfelues , and laſtly to be
depriued euen of the paffiue alfo,
fo farr as it may feeme fēfible vnto
the foule,that it is her own work.
And this to the end that Gods wil
may be the pure and only motiue
of her will and workes whatfoeuer. Thou muſt beware in thefe
& the like fentences, of two feue-
rall doᶜtrines or errors , wholy
contrary to that which is heere
intended. The one , leaſt thou
thinke that a foule being come to
that eſtate , doth not indeed work
with her owne will,but that God
then worketh all in her , fo that
thofe workes be not really the a-
ᶜtions of the foule, but of God
him•

himselfe, which thing is both
false and absurd. The other er-
ror is, that a soule in this state of
Perfection should not doe any
thing, but as seing her selfe to be
cleerly moued therunto by the
will of God, and in a manner
compelled by the same to doe all
her actiōs, so that she in the mean
tyme should be idle, vntill she
feele this impulsion from God.
This doctrine would nourish
slouth in the soule, yea and breed,
if not bring forth, heresy also
against the freedome of our will,
and against the necessitie of our
concurrence with the grace of
God : all which are not different
only, but contrary to the intention of the Author, as (besides
the authority of the *Parisian* Do-
ctours who approued this book,
it being translated out of Italian,

to set it forth in their owne lan-
guage) the diligent & impartiall
Reader may alto by himself eafily
difcern, if he mark wel the whole
difcourfe. For he fhall find it here
required, that ore omit no practife, or proofe of likely meanes,
either in rooting out of euill, or
in planting of good habits : alfo
that all the rules, & aduifes of this
booke, are to be applied to euery
mans eftate, and that he omit-
ting no part of his dutie, doe
practife the fame, togeather with
the actions which his eftate and
inftitute require . Laftly that this
Subtraction of actiue and paffiue
will, touching the acts of vertue,
is the worke only of God in the
foule with which(whē the foule
doth perceaue it to be fo) it muft
concurre as with the will of God
to will the fame thing, as our
dutie

dutie doth bind vs . And this is
no other thing then we find in
daily practife , though all doe
not feele it a like, nor all follow
this rule, as they fhould , when
they feele it . Yt happeneth vnto
vs more or leſſe whenſoeuer any
deſolation by Gods appointment
doth fall vpon vs , for in that
caſe we finde our ſelues leſſe apt
then before to will or worke any
good, yea, or to ſuffer the procee-
ding of that goud (which before
we deſired) with any contentment; and this deſolation may ſo
increaſe , that it ſhall ſeeme to vs,
our deſire carrieth vs wholy to
the contrary of that we had reſolued. But all this is only in the inferiour part of our ſoule , to wit ,
in our naturall inclinatiõ, which
for the time is left to it ſelf by
Subtraction of that effect and fruit
of

of grace, by which it was before
comforted, ſtrengthened, and
enabled to performe good actiõs,
and concur to ſupernaturall vertues, with deſire and delight:
which to be the effectes and fruits
of grace, the Apoſtle reacheth,
Galat. 5. 22. when he ſaith: *Fru-*
ctus autem ſpiritus eſt charitas, gaudium,
pax, patientia &c. So that all this
while grace is not diminiſhed
in the ſuperiour part of the ſoule
nor the vertues leſſe perfect which
are placed therin, but only the
redoundance, fruit, and effect of
that grace is ſtopped, and ſubtra-
cted for the time, from the inferiour part, to increaſe the battaile
which the ſoule is to haue, and
ſo the victory which it is to obtaine by conſtantly confirming
and vniting her will to Gods,
notwithſtanding that increaſed
diffi-

difficultie , yea by renouncing
her owne naturall will and inclination, transforming the fame
into the will of God, and fo faying with our Sauiour Chrift in
the like cafe : *Non mea, fed tua voluntas fiat , Pater,* not my will, o Father , but thine be donne . In
whofe example we may fee, that
the practife of this point may
ftand with all Perfection, which
could not be wanting in his a-
ctions. So that the fcope of this
doctrine is not to make vs idle
or remiffe in working , nor to
expect that God fhould doe all in
vs , and that our will fhould haue
no part in the action : but it requireth, that we doe cooperate
with Gods grace , and labour
with all diligéce, whileft we can,
and when by Gods ordinance
we feele that our fenfible force
doth

doth faile vs , and that we are
not now able to creep, who before were able to runne in the
wayes of God (as the Prophet
saith , *Pſal* . 118. 32.) *cùm dilataret
cor noſtrum*, whilest he dilated our
hart with ioy and comfort: we
must then conforme our will to
God , yea , and be glad to tranſ-
forme our weake will into his
strength of goodnes, to vnite our
drop of water to his ſea of graces,
and to ſay with our actiue will
(though our inclinations striue
against it) that his will ſhall be
ours, and the more that we deſire
his will may be done with vs in
all thinges , howſoeuer our inferiour part doe according to nature, deſire the contrary .

This is the Perfection vnto
which this booke leadeth : the
practiſe whereof we may ſee
both

both vſed and declared by God
to his beloued Apoſtle, as may be
gathered out of the firſt Chapter
of the 2. *Epiſt . Cor* . and it is the
higheſt which the ſoule can arriue vnto in this life. For as the
will of God is infinitly good,
and euen goodnes it ſelf , ſo the
nearer we come vnto it, the more
we approach to a good and perfect eſtate. Neyther can there be
euen by imagination conceaued,
a higher Perfection , or greater
happines, either in this world or
the next, then to be vnited vnto
God, the fountaine of all goodnes. In this life it is to be dõne
by grace , and in the next by
glorie . This litle booke, gentle
Reader, will lead thee to the one,
and thy diligent practiſe of what
it teacheth will bring thee to the
other.

Chriſt

To the Reader .

Chrift IESVS graunt vs grace to feeke this treafure with true defire, and finding it, to vfe it to our beft commoditie . We fhall doe it the better, if we pray hartily one for another , which I purpofe to doe for all , that will endeauour to practife this Booke, and do craue the like of them for my greater needs. Fare-well .

TO

TO
THE SOVLES
TRVLY VNITED
VNTO GOD,

AND

enlightened with his diuine
brightnes and light, moſt
humble ſalutations .

*M OST deare ſpouſes of Ie-
ſus Chriſt, ſome while agoe
this little booke was tranſ-
ſlated by the diligence of a
certaine Gaſcoyne Gentle-
man out of Italian into French; but for
that it was found after the impreſſion ſo
full of wants, omiſſions, obſcurities, and
faults in many places therof, that it could
hardly be drawne to any good ſenſe : many
perſons of rare vertue, and well experien-*

A 2   *ced*

ced in mysticall diuinity, iudged it a great
detriment, that so excellent a treasure
should be thus hid, and clouded in so great
darknes. For this booke how little soeuer it
seemes, treateth of most high, and admirable perfection, and most expediēt for
the spirituall profit of a Christiā soule, according to the iudgmēt of thē, that are well
experiēced in this sacred diuinity: & there
is scarce any to be found in these times
more worthy, nor of greater profit, if we
regard the subiect wherof it treateth. For
which cause men of great learning and
excellent knowledg in spirituall matters,
of diuers Orders, haue carefully laboured
to correct it, to make cleare the darke
places therof, and restore many passages
to their proper sense, which were before
corrupted and obscure, that so being
published, it might appeare worthy to
be presented to your sights, and to the
view of all posterity. This is a packet,
deuout Soules, addressed principally vnto
you. Heere are letters shut vp from the
learned

*learned - ignorant , and wise of the
world. This booke is sealed from them
with seauen seales, like vnto that which
was shewed vnto S . Iohn , as is recor-
ded in his Reuelations, and there is none
but the Lambe; your deare Spouse, that
can open it , and the holy Spirit proceding
eternally from the heauenly Father, and
from his diuine wisdome .*

*For this cause therefore we pray you
most humbly , that it be not communica-
ted to such as are vncapable : following
the aduertisment which our Sauiour giueth vs , that we giue not holy things vnto
doggs , nor cast pearles before swine. For
this cause* S . Denys *Bishop of* Athens
and Apostle of France, *writing certaine
secrets of this aforesaid mysticall diuinity
to his deare friend.* Timothy *Bishop of*
Ephesus , *saith :* His autem , vide,
quomodo nemo indoctorum au-
scultet : *Take heed, that those that are
ignorant ,vncapable,and vnworthy of this
holy doctrine, heare not this. And truly he*
A 3   *said*

said very well: for the vessell of election
S. Paul *his happy Maister, and spiritu-*
all father, who had first begotten him in
Iesus Christ, *witnesseth, that* animalis
homo non percipit ea, quæ sunt
spiritus Dei: *The carnall, or world-*
ly man cannot vnderstand nor compre-
hend heauenly and diuine things, that pro-
ceed from the spirit of God.

 Moreouer we desire you not to make
the lesse accompt of this worke, though
the Authors name be not put in the begin-
ning therof, according as the holy and sa-
cred Councell of Trent *hath ordained, &*
the rules of the new Catalogue of the Books
prohibited, and censured by our holy Fa-
ther the Pope do require: for as yet we
could not certainly learne the name of
him, or her that made it, though the com-
mon opinion is, that it came out of the clo-
set of a most vertuous and honorable Lady
of Millain, *indued with rare and excel-*
lent perfection. All that is written in this
Booke resembleth rather the spirit of a S.
        Denis,

Denis, *or of a* S . Catherine *of Si-*
ena,then the fraile and weak vnderstan-
ding of a simple woman . But our Lord
chooseth often the infirme of this world,
to confound the strong, and reproueth the
vayne wisdome of worldly men . And our
holy father, and the sacred Councell a-
foresaid, doth not absolutely forbid good
books of Catholicke Authors whose names
are vnknown,so they be approued by some
Doctors in Diuinity : & therfore it is not
for this cause to be the lesse esteemed, or
iudged vnworthy to be published to the
world .

VVe had a great desire to haue dedi-
cated it to some worthy spirituall Man, or
VVoman of nobility,from whome such ex-
cellent & most odoriferous flowers of ver-
tue do proceed , as may rauish the harts,
& minds of the beholders,& bring them
into no small admiration:but their mode-
sty , & humility hath hindred vs, being
more desirous to haue their names writtē
in heauē, then read in earth, saying in the

A 4 *depth*

depth of their hart, Secretum meum mihi, secretum meum mihi: *My secret to my self, my secret to my self. But the more they desire to be vnknowne to the world, so much the more cleare doth our Lord make their vertues knowne to his elect, and to those that are guided with the self same spirit with them. He that prayeth vnto God in the sincerity of his hart for the whole world, prayeth no lesse for all, thē he that prayeth seuerally for e-uery one, & his praier shal be so much the more excellent before God, by how much lesse subiect it is to distraction: and as he also that seeth a great troope of people to-geather, seeth them aswell, as if he saw euery one, one after another: so in our iudgment we do no lesse, dedicating this Booke to all holy Soules in generall, then if we had dedicated it only to some one in particuler. For* S. Denis *before named, witnesseth in the booke*, Of diuine Names, Bonum quò longiùs ma-nat, cò præstabilius, *the more that a good*

good thing is common, so much is it more excellent, and diuine.

Receaue then, you chaſt Spouſes of Ieſus Chriſt, this little preſent, which we dedicate vnto you in generall, in no leſſe affectuous a manner, then if we did the ſame in particuler to euery one alone. Receaue it with as good a will on your parts, as we preſent it vnto you : Beſeeching you moſt humbly, to be mindfull of vs in your holy praiers, and deuotions, at leaſtwiſe thē, when as you ſhall be ſtraitly imbraced with the holy imbracings of your moſt loyall, and moſt faithfull Bridegrome; or when you ſhall be abſorpt, & as it were drowned in that deepe, and large Ocean of his bounty and mercy, which hath neither end nor limit; or els when you ſhall haue obteined to that moſt high, and excellent degree of holy quietnes, wherof is made mention in this little diſcourſe. And on our parts we ſhall pray vnto his diuine Maieſty, although our prayers be very poore, and moſt vnworthy,

worthy, that it will please him to im-
part vnto you, increase of his holy graces,
and to lighten you more and more, with
his diuine brightnes. From Paris *this*
thirteenth of Iuly 1598. *by those that*
desire infinitly to remaine al-
wayes, and euer

Your more then most humble
seruants in Iesus Christ,

D . C . M .

A N

AN ABRIDGMENT OF CHRISTIAN PERFECTION.

VVHAT PERFECTION ought to be presupposed in the soule that entreth into the practise of that which is treated of in this discourse.

CHAP. I.

THIS Perfection requi-
reth a firme & resolute
desire in the soule that
vndertaketh it, and a
determinate and setled
purpose to attaine vnto
it, and aboue all, it must be, as the

white

white at which she aymeth, and
the end which she pretendeth in all
her actions. It requireth also that
she giue her selfe to mortification of
her senses, and passions, endeauouring to subdue the repugnance and
contradiction which riseth of them, &
to obtaine full dominion and victory
ouer them. Moreouer that she apply
her selfe wholy to the mortification, &
abnegation of her wil, & proper iudgment; vnder an entire obedience & a
full direction of her Superiour, euen
with all the forces of her soulē. That
likewise she so apply her self to vertue
according to the occasions occurring,
or in any other sort; and principally
to charity, to the loue of God and her
neihgbour, that she be not in this way
alwaies rude, and as a beginner, but
well aduanced and profited by progresse of time; at the least she must haue
attained a firme resolution, to be willing rather to dye, then to offend God,
yea although but venially, or to commit one of the least defects against perfection, in such sort, that the sinne she
doth

doth commit, be by meere occurring
frailty. The cauſe wherefore all this
that hath byn ſaid, ought to be preſuppoſed, is, for that a firme purpoſe of
all theſe things in generall, is moſt neceſſary for the obtaining of Perfeſtion.
And it is certaine that whoſoeuer without a very earneſt deſire of theſe things
doth with coldnes, and negligence
ſeeke after vertue, giuing himſelfe to
his proper commodities, and ſelfe intereſts, liuing like a libertine, and
with a will to remaine in his old habits, without amendment; can neuer
attaine, nor come neere to Perfeſtion,
and much leſſe to this that is the higheſt of all.

TWO PRINCIPLES
in which conſiſteth Perfeſtion.

CHAP. II.

ALL the building of ſo high Perfeſtion is founded in theſe two
Principles, which conſiſt in praſtice:

ctice: and therfore by the vse of them, being attentiue to the daily actions of his vocation, and inſtitution, aſſuredly he ſhall come to the toppe, and full height of all his building. The firſt principle is, to haue a meane & a baſe eſteeme of things created, & aboue all of himſelfe, frō which eſteeme ought to be deriued at leaſt in affectiō, an entire forſaking of all creatures, & a renouncing of himſelfe. And cōcerning his affection, to haue alwaies this firme in his will & reſolution, but to put it in practiſe principally, when it is needful. And from this ought to be deriued alſo a true knowledg of the withdrawing that God worketh in vs, admitting, & accepting it, with a ready wil, to wit, to content our ſelues, and with great ioy of hart to accept it, when our Lord retireth himſelfe a little from vs, or depriueth vs of any thing whatſoeuer.

The ſecond Principle is to haue a moſt high eſteeme of God, not by the way of penetration with Theological conceipts, or the like high pointes of Diui-

Diuinity, for this few can reach vnto, & it is not neceſſary: but rather by the meane of a great promptitude, & entire ſubmiſſion of the will, & of the whole man, to the maieſty of God, to adore him, & to do whatſoeuer he exacteth of vs, for his greater glory, without any intereſt of ours, how holy ſoeuer it be. For which eſteeme it ſufficeth, that the ſoule with the light of faith apprehend God (as we are taught in our Creed) as Almighty, the ſoueraigne good, our end: & that for the great loue he bare vnto vs, he was moued to make himſelfe man, to ſuffer paines & death for our ſakes. Moreouer that he is alwaies preſent with vs & in al things gouerneth vs, as wel in thoſe of nature, as of grace: & in particuler calleth vs with a ſingular vocation, to labour for ſo high Perfectiõ, & the like; which ſpeciall fauours our Lord giueth to euery one conformable to his capacity, and according to the meaſure of grace.

Of this ſo excellent, and high eſteeme, ought to ſpring a full and entire

tire conformity with the diuine will,
which alwayes muft be the rule of all
our defignements, affections and daily operations. This maner of working
by the forfaid meane, with the vfe of
thefe two Principles, bringeth the
foule to the vnion, and transforma-
tion in God, which is called Deificatiõ,
not by the myfticall way of rauifhing
out of our fenfes, and eleuation of the
vnderftanding, nor by moft vehement
affections, that are deriued, and proceed frõ thence; for this is fubiect to a
thoufand illufions, and to great labour,
with danger of infirmity of body, &
ruine of fpirit, and fuch paine for the
moft part auaileth little, and few do attaine vnto it : But it is by the beaten
and common way, to wit, by the will
wholy conformed, and with great fta-
bility trãsformed into the diuine Wil,
by perfect loue, the which maketh it
to worke all in God, and for God euen
without light : & of this all are capable, & any that wil, may come vnto it
with ioy, and comfort, but yet not
without paine and labour. And after
this

this there followeth ordinarily many
other giftes of light, and diuine affections, but they are to be taken as graces that are giuen *gratis* , as truly they
are, and we ought not to be too careful
for them or to rely much vpon them.
They are diuers according to the variety of foules, to fome more , to o-
thers leffe ; and there is no rule on our
part , but all dependeth of God , and
ought to be wholy fubmitted to his
diuine pleafure .

OF THE FIRST
Eftate : and firft of Anibilation .

CHAP. III.

THE forefaid principles applied
to the diuerfities of our occafiõs,
actions , and motions , do make
the foule to walke with continual progreffe , from the beginning, euen vnto
the end of Perfection , and all is redu-
ced into three eftates , euery one of
which , and principally the firft , con-
                                    taineth

taineth diuers degrees, that maketh
the foule mount, as it were, by certaine degrees, going from one eftate
vnto another, euen to the laft. In the
firft eftate, the foule walketh by the
way of the knowledge, & bafe efteeme
of her felfe, which is done in diuers
manners, and principally in foure.

1. The firft is in acknowledging, &
efteeming herfelfe purely nothing, feing that of nothing fhe was created, &
fhould be conuerted into nothing of
her felfe, if God did not conferue her.
Vnto which it helpeth much, to com-
pare herfelfe to the whole world, to
all men, to heauen, to Saints, and to
God himfelfe, in refpect of which
things, fhe knoweth herfelfe to be not
fo much as a little drop of water, cõ-
pared with the fea.

2. Secondly in houlding herfelfe for
the moft vile, & vnprofitable creature
of all, how vile foeuer they be, as is
duft, a finke, an Apoftume &c. all
thefe things being good for fome vfe,
but fhe for nothing, but to offẽd God.

3. Thirdly in thinking herfelfe the
grea-

greateſt ſinner in the world , yea greater then all the diuels put togeather,
and worthy of more chaſtiſment , attributing to herſelfe all the ſinnes that
are committed , and that all their tor-
mentes duly might be inflicted vpon
her . For there is no ſinne but ſhe
might haue cōmitted it, if God had not
preſerued her: examples of this may be
ſeene in the liues of *S. Francis* and *S.
Catherine* of *Siena* .

4. The fourth conſiſteth in this, that
ſhe ought to deſcend to the knowledg
of the thinges of the world , the better
to contemne them : and for the reiecting of them , ſhe muſt make choice
of the vileſt and baſeſt of them , as cōcerning her place, garments , and any
thing els; yet ſo notwithſtanding, that
ſhe affect not ſingularity: and ſhe muſt
eſteeme the moſt abiect corner in the
houſe the fitteſt habitation for her ; &
that the office or charge ſhe hath , ex-
ceedeth much her merits; and that ſhe
is not worthy of them , much leſſe of
greater . The foreſaid practice bringeth a man to a true anihilation of him
ſelfe.

felfe . And although he doth not apprehend fuch conceipts in his vnder-
ftanding , as may clearely reprefent
fuch bafenes vnto him , as he would;
yet doth not he leaue to haue that e-
fteeme of himfelf, feeing that he , who
willingly abafeth himfelfe, and pre-
ferreth all creatures , how vile foeuer
they be , before him , éfteemeth and
reputeth himfelfe alwaies the leaft: and
he that knoweth not the practife of
this anihilation , knoweth not the profit , and commodity therof.

Thirdly in the foule that is founded thus in her owne nothing , there
followeth alfo the difappropriation or
true abnegation , the fubtraction or
withdrawing that God accuftometh to
worke in the foule, & the conformity
with the diuine will , which maketh a
man to be transformed into God , and
thefe things as they haue diuers obiects,
fo they haue diuers degrees , according
to the order that followeth .

O P

OF THE FIRST
*degree of Abnegation , Subtraction ,
Conformity : & of the Abiecti-
on , and Anihilation of
himselfe .*

CHAP. IIII.

FIRST , and principally there is
wrought in the foule a full , and
entire renunciation of all things
created , that are indifferent , as life ,
death, health, all commodities , taft &
intereft of them , offices , dignities ,
poffeffions , and other the like things:
and this is to be done , firft with the
affection , renouncing them entirely,
& all defire or will , fhe may haue of
them : & for her owne part, fhe ought
to caft of all defire , and affection , &
intention that fhe may haue therin ,
and the hopes of any commodity ,
taft & pleafure that may be had therby , euen as if fhe were dead .

Secondly by worke , leauing
actually

actually that which is superfluous, &
retaining only that which is needfull
to her, according to her ftate, with the
counfaile, & confent of her Superiour.
To this doth correfpond the fubtraction, or withdrawing, that God doth
in vs of the like things: to wit, of life
by fending vs death, of health, by
vifiting vs with ficknes, of commodities and meanes when they are take
from vs, of pleafures and folaces, fending vs paines : & finally of any other
worldly change, wherof we haue experience almoft euery houre. All being
done by the diuine prouidence in
fuch fort, that there paffeth not any
day, in which our Lord doth not take
from vs, and depriue vs (according
to the variety of his prouidence) of
many obiects, and commodities,
concerning thefe tranfitory, & fading
things. And he that is free from all
affection to the like things, admitteth
with great alacrity all priuation of
them, & eafily contemneth them all,
how great foeuer they be.

Likewife to this fubtraction, &
priuation

priuation correspondeth a meruailous cōformity with the diuine Will, not desiring any created thing whatso-euer, but that which our Lord wil-leth, and that which he giueth vs, reioycing to be, by the meanes of these changes & varieties, continually depriued of them by his fatherly boū-ty: & euen those things, that he besto-weth vpon vs, we ought not desire to haue them, but only for that his wil is so, hauing no regard to our par-ticuler interest, commodity, desire & affection, but only to the greatest glo-ry of God : not seruing our selues, or vsing any thing, but conformable to the diuine Wil, manifested vnto vs by the wil, & ordinances of our Supe-riour, & according to our manner of lyuing .

The practice of all this consisteth, first in a totall indifferency in respect of things created, as we haue set downe for the foundation of our exercises . Secondly to make election of an estate conformable to Gods wil; & if already we haue done so, we must choose in
the

the māner of liuing therin the bafeſt,
and moſt abieſt, praying & working
continually with the felfe fame rules
of our exerciſes. Thirdly to exerciſe
in all our dayly operatiōs the vertues
according to their occurēts, to wit, tē-
perāce, patience, & the like, with abnegation, ſubtraſtion, & eleſtion, already ſpokē of, by which means the vertues we do (eſpecially if we conforme
them to the diuine Wil, & do them
for his glory, and honour) come to be
more noble, more perfeſt, & excellent
then before. The fourth conſiſteth in
a totall dependance of the prouidēce,
and wil of God, in all that he giueth
vs, or taketh frō vs of any thing created. Fiftly in offering our felues during our praier, and out of the fame
entirely, and fully vnto God.

By all theſe exerciſes there is increaſed in the foule with the foreſaid
conformity, a very great, & true loue
of God, feing there is takē away al the
hinderance of any created thing, that
was betwene God & the foule. And
by this meanes the foule commeth to
vnite

vnite herselfe perfectly with her Creator, & to transforme her self perfectly
into him : from vvhich ordinarily followeth great gifts, as lights, affections,
and diuine motions: but for these we
are not to be much carefull, but to
seeke aboue all, to separate our selues
with all our power frō created things,
and wholy to resigne our selues vnto God . And this is the extasy , and
rauishing of the will , and not of the
vnderstanding , which is much greater, and higher, and which Deifieth the
soule more .

THE SECOND

Degree.

Chap . V .

VV E ought to passe further in
subtraction , or withdrawing our selues from things
created . For not only this subtraction ought to be of indifferent thinges,
as is said , but also of holy and spiri-
tu-

tuall, that are meanes to vnite the spirit with God; yet not as of such, must we depriue our selues of them, but for so much as vnder the colour of holines, there may be hid proper loue, and particuler interest; and of these there is to be noted many degres. The first and that which is commonly vnderstood of spirituall men to be the lowest, or basest, is touching spirituall consolations, redounding euen to the affections of the hart, that are sensitiue to wit, tendernes, feruour, teares, sweetnes in our operations, & great facility surmounting difficulties, by abondance of spirituall delight: of which things we ought to depriue our selues, and not to cease vntil such time, as we haue no more feeling of any desire to them.

The depriuing our selues of these, consisteth in not making any esteeme, or any accompt of them, considering that these facilities, that induce vs to worke, proceed not of any habit, or particuler gifts or graces nor principally of charity; but only of this sweetnes

nes and pleafure taken therin, which
is an obiect very proportionate to felf-
loue, and particuler intereft, which
nourifheth it felfe with felfe contentment, and pleafure that commeth in
tyme vnto a fpirituall gluttony: and to
receaue fatisfaction in this, or to make
any great efteeme therof, is no other
thing,the to conuert holy obiects into
our delights and pleafures, and abufe
holy things ,accommodating them to
our guft, and feeling . A very great
vice, although it be fecret and hid ,
from which eafily may fpring diuers
vaine delightes, proud illufions, and
diabolicall deceipts,and a thoufand o-
ther euils . Alfo we muft not thinke
that vertue dependeth of them or confifteth therin, but we muft know, that
this is a childifh thing, and that with
this fweetnes & facility,a litle ftrength
and vertue is fufficient to make vs
imbrace the hardeft, and moft difficult matters therfore we muft depriue our felues of all defire of them
as of a meane thing, & of little e-
fteme: and by the forefaid anihilation,

B 2   ac-

acknowledge our selues most vnworthy of them, with a totall indifference to haue them or not, being incited by vertue and perfection, to vse them when we haue them, only for the end that God sendeth them, to wit, acknovvledging them with great submission, and referring them vnto God, from vvhome they proceed, directing in them our intention to establish vs, and to increase so much the more in true & solide vertues: taking alwaies heed least that transported, and made drunk vvith this svvetnes and spirituall tast, vve do not make purposes, or dangerous promises of vertues, or workes that surpasse our forces, and which, when that sensible delight and pleasure ceaseth, will seeme most difficult, yea impossible vnto vs.

And to auoid such danger, the submission already spoken of helpeth greatly; that is, when vve admit with great promptitude of hart, the taking away of such consolations as God is accustomed at times to take from vs, and then to make greater estimation

of

of God, and of vertue, then of any
such consolations, yet labouring still
according to those former motions,
with a greater, and more ardent desire
then euer, without hauing regard to
the contentment of self-loue, but only
to the loue of vertue it selfe, and for
the diuine glory.

The conformity with God here is
cleare, and is of great importance, for
that to vnite himselfe with the diuine
will, he depriueth himselfe on his part
of such consolation, contenting himselfe with his spirituall crosse whatsoeuer it be; and so much the more, for
that such tafts, and motions surpasse
all things created, and all the pleasures
that they can affoard and how much
the more a man depriueth himselfe in
this sort; so much the more he tranf-
formeth himselfe into God, and perfect loue, and Deification increaseth in
him.

THE THIRD
Degree.

CHAP. VI.

AFTER the forefaid degree, there
is accuftomed to fucceed & de-
fcend into the foule celeftiall
lights, defires, and affections of ftable
and folid vertues, that are without cō-
parifon much more high thē the fwetnes already fpoken of; for that they
are moft effectuall meanes for getting
of the faid folid and ftable vertues, &
haue their being in the fuperiour part
of man. And then the foule ought to
mount to the higheft degree of forfaking and renouncing his owne will, &
of fubtraction, and conformity to the
diuine will, with the help of the anihilation, & humble efteeme aforefaid.

Therfore it is neceffary to be aduertifed, that although fuch lights,
and affections be from God in the beginning, and that prefently vpon the
recei-

receiuing, & imbracing of them, they
produce in the soule excellent effects
mouing and inciting it to vnite her self
with God, by the meanes of firme &
solid vertues: neuertheles soone after
if a man be not well aduised, but suffer himselfe to proceed according to
his naturall inclination, ordinarily he
will imbrace willingly such lights, and
affections, with a certaine satisfaction, and a very great contentement in
himself: which is a hidden delight of
himselfe in them: & to cooperate with
such lights, he setteth himselfe to dif-
course at large, and to fortifie the naturall forces of his vnderstanding, wil,
and affections, with the which it seemeth vnto him, that his first lights
much increase, & are interiourly dilated: which yet is not so, neither is it
any effect of God, but only a pure reflection of the soule, and a great contentement and pleasure, which she taketh of their first beginning.

And thus by little and little, the in-
fusion of such lights coming to cease,
the naturall, and reasonable strength

of

of the foule remaineth alone, which
ordinarily is felf-loue, which by this
delight goeth dilating this little that he
hath of diuine light, esteeming that to
be very great which is not: and in this
fort he falleth into blindnes of pride,&
vaine perfwafion of great vertue, frō
whēce do fpring a thoufand falfhoods,
deceipts, & illufions; our Lord withdrawing his hand, becaufe of the barre
of felf-loue which man hath put in his
way: and yet fuch do thinke that they
haue great grace infufed,& great light,
and it is nothing (the beginning only
excepted) but only difcourfe, and naturall ftrength. And in the end, abandoned of the diuine influence, they
fall into great faults, & errours; and
from hence oftentimes proceed very
great illufiōs, which notwithftanding
had a good beginning.

Prefently therfore when the foule
receaueth fuch motions, fhe ought to
humble, and anihilate her felfe with
great fubmiffion, euen as nothing,
And this act rooteth out, and cutteth
off all the force of this delight already
                                    fpo-

ſpoken of . Afterwards ſhe muſt pro-
teſt , that ſhe will not ſeeke any ſelfe-
contentment , reputing her ſelfe moſt
vnworthy , as a moſt vile and abiect
perſon ; and this to free her foule of al
ſelfe-loue , which by reaſon of ſuch
lights may enter into it . And here ſhe
depriueth herſelfe of a much more noble thing then before : & by this greater vertue is obtained. And although
it ſeeme vnto her that ſhe diminiſheth,
or decreaſeth , yet notwithſtanding it
is not ſo , but the hinderance is taken
away that kept the ſoule back , & did
hurt her greatly . And our Lord finding the ſoule by ſuch abnegation diſpoſed , increaſeth with his particuler
concourſe , the like lights and motiôs ,
by true and ſolid meanes , although it
be not with ſo great taſt , & pleaſure ,
and guideth her with great ſafety in
the way of Perfection .

The ſoule thus depriued by the
meanes of ſuch pure & diuine lights,
commeth to refer and attribute them
vnto God, feeling her ſelt in them affected only to the diuine glory , and

not vnto any other thing, with great
acknowledgment of the diuine bouty,
vvho vouchſafeth by diuine infuſions,
to abaſe himſelf to ſo vile a thing. And
this rule of ſpirituall motions is a matter of great importance : for that, if
they be not of God, preſẽtly they wil
be diſcouered by this abnegation ; and
if ſuch lights come from God, we ſhal
be ſecured,that neither ſelfe loue, nor
the diuell can haue any part in them.
And moreouer referring them vnto
God, who hath giuen them vnto vs,
we come to make more eſteeme of the
giuer, then of the gifts, and by this
meanes get true and ſolid vertue.

There followeth afterwards another conformity of moſt pure lights,
and motions, with the act of the will,
and affections, purged from all ſelfe-
reſpect, and veſted with the diuine
will, pretending in ſuch diuine influ-
ences only to obey Almighty God, &
his diuine pleaſure, and nothing our
ſelues, where with the ſoule paſſeth into God, & transformeth her ſelfe more
highly, and profoundly then euer ; &
here

here she offereth, & giueth, and de-
dicateth her self wholy vnto God.

THE FOVRTH
Degree.

CHAP. VII.

AFTER that the soule is exerci-
sed thus in purging & disappro-
priating her selfe in these spirituall motions, and in desire of solid
vertue, as hath byn said: there will
follow a higher degree which is this.
It happeneth often, that hauing such
desires, the soule cannot attaine vnto
that she pretendeth, and that for some
worldly, or humane cause which doth
hinder it: as for example, when we
must leaue prayer, by the which the
soule findeth her selfe prompt, apt,
ready, & as it were inuited to vnite
her self with God. And obedience on
the other side, or charity requireth to
leaue it for another worke of great distraction, but profitable to our neigh-
bours. And this wilbe necessary not

B 6   only

only in one worke, or at one tyme only, but it shalbe needful also cocerning our manner of liuing, to leaue the quiet, & contemplatiue life, in which the soule felt her selfe greatly inflamed with ardent desire of solid vertues to busy herselfe in the negotiations of the actiue life, in which she shal haue great repugnance, and by which she shal receaue many occasions or distraction; neuertheles she seeth clearely, that she is called by God to leaue that for this, and some tymes also shall find hinderances which proceed frō God, to wit, when God giueth vs not so quickly as we vvould, this vertue and perfection, which he inciteth vs to desire.

In the like occasions the soule is accustomed to feele paine, anxiety, & sorrow, for such hinderances, and is therewith much afflicted. It is needfull here that she consider, that there may be selfe-interest in this busines, although it be very secret, and hidden, which she ought to cast away wholy, with a noble & couragious abnegatiō.

The sorrow then, and anxiety
that

that afflicteth the foule in fuch defires
and maketh it vnquiet , proceedeth
ordinarily of felf loue : and although
it be without finne , neuertheleffe it is
a hinderance betweene God , and the
foule ; feing that as a thing created . it
hindereth perfection , and keepeth
the foule back from arriuing to the top
of the fame. Alfo the propriety is dif-
couered plainely, although it be of a
holy thing,and it feemeth therby (although indirectly) that a man will
giue a law vnto God . And finally the
vnquietnes that afflicteth the foule inwardly , is not of God , whofe fpirit
is fweet and gratious,and full of peace
and tranquillity : and to take away
fuch vnquietnes, he muft forfake fuch
defires , and the vertue it felf , in the
manner that followeth .

Firft a man ought to accept , and
receiue this defire as a gift of God ,
without refting or ftaying himfelf in
his proper delight and fatisfaction , as
hath bene faid in the degree before :
and he ought to procure with all diligence to put it in execution,neuer letting

ting paſſe any meanes, that he doth
not try by experience, & put in practice, that therby he may come to ſuch
vertue and perfection: for ſo much as
doing this, he chaſeth far away all tepidity, and negligence.

When theſe hinderances before
declared happen, he ought preſently
to thinke that the diuine bounty is
not pleaſed at that time in the execution of his deſire, and therfore he ought
to renounce it quite, with proteſtati-
on that he will haue neyther vertue,
nor perfection(I meane, the executiõ,
or act of deſire only, for the ground
or eſſence of the deſire ought to remaine) but euen ſuch, and in that
manner, and when God will giue it;
renouncing vtterly all the reſt. He
ought then to take away all anxiety,
and griefe, diſcouering plainely his
ſelfe-loue, and his owne intereſt, that
was hid vnder ſuch deſires, although
they be holy: and alſo learne this moſt
high doctrine, which is, that ſuch a
deſire euen of martyrdome, with this
anxiety, although it ſeeme to be a
                              great

great thing, commeth to be very baſe,
and little, forſomuch as it is ſelfe-inte-
reſt , & a hinderance betweene God,
and the ſoule : which being taken a-
vvay, the deſire remaineth as great as
euer , and inſteed of the anxiety , it is
accompanied vvith a meruailous tranquillity in God , & in his diuine Will.

And note vvell, that the ſoule that
hath ſuch a deſire vvith repoſe , & trā-
quillity, vvithout the vertue & perfe-
ctiō deſired, is more agreeable to God
thē any other vvho hath ſuch a vertue,
which if ſhe had not receaued , or had
not attayned vnto , would haue beene
much grieued , and troubled : ſeeing
that he obtayneth moſt perfection ,
vvho is moſt conformed to Gods wil,
and pleaſure , and exchangeth the vertue created, for the diuine will increated , vvhich doth farre ſurpaſſe ; and
infinitely exceed the other : notwithſtanding the deſire vvil remaine , not
vvith humane feare , that afflicteth &
diſquieteth the ſoule , but vvith a diuine feare , vvhich is annexed neceſſa-
rily vnto the deſire . For to deſire a
thing

thing that we cannot haue, bringeth feare, which is accompanied with paine, vntill fuch time as it is obtay- ned : but this is a paine from the which doth proceed a meruailous content- ment, and a refignation vnto God, knowing wel that our Lord is pleafed greatly vvith fuch a paine, to wit, to fee a foule quiet, and full of peace in her paine, to refigne her felf & accoplifh his vvil, vvho for to pleafe her Lord, wil- lingly and of her owne accord, wil re- maine depriued of a good, that fhe fo inftantly doth defire, becaufe her loue vnto her Lord, is more then vnto any perfection, or vertue.

In fuch a foule remaineth ordina- rily a diuine light, that doth inftruct and teach her, what great diligence fhe ought to vfe, without euer relen- ting, or waxing cold and negligent; but a foule muft not rely vpon the fame, feeing fhe doth not come to this that fhe defireth by her diligence, & induftry, how great foeuer it be, but by the will and pleafure of God, who fometimes giueth it, and fometimes not

not, euen as he best pleaseth. Therefore by reiecting, and loosing all esteeme of our owne diligence, and industry, is gotten a certaine confidence
and filiall security, that God, who
hath giuen the desire, will also giue
the perfection, when he shall please,
and according to his vvill . And thus
for his ovvne part, the soule putteth,
and casteth herselfe as a little infant into his armes, and is most contented
withall, thinking no more of it, but
with a pure and sincere resignation vnto God, worketh as out of her selfe,
and, as vve may say, at aduenture
leaueth all care of her selfto our Lord,
as a little infant, vvith a kind of diuine tranquillity.

To this so high renunciation, &
disappropriation doth correspond the
subtraction, or withdrawing of our
Lord already spoken of , when he
doth not giue the vertue we demand,
which we ought to admit with ioy,
and cooperate in the manner aforesaid. Also there is discouered clearely
a conformity with the diuine will, very

ry secret, and knovvne but vnto few,
seing that a man leaueth God for God,
that is to say, leaueth and renounceth
God, in as much as he bringeth any
selfe interest with vertue, and perfection, to haue him more excellent-
ly, to wit, without any interest. From
whence follovveth a most high trans-
formation, and an admirable Deification, from which is accustomed to
proceed excellent gifts, and very rare
lights, vvorthy of such a loue, and so
great vnion vvith God.

In particuler the aforesaid doctrine
ought to be applied to three sorts of
desires, besides the place it hath in all
others. The first is of eternall glory,
in vvhich she ought to be resigned in
the manner before specified, vvhen
our Lord deferreth it, esteeming
much more of the diuine vvill, to
the end she might entirely forsake all
selfe loue, although it be of the most
excellent good that is.

The second is the desire of this a-
nihilation, renouncing of her selfe, &
conformity vvith God, vvhich she
                                        must

muſt alſo moderate with the ſelf ſame
rule aforeſaid, when our Lord doth
not giue it ſo much as ſhe would :
where is meruailouſly perceiued, that
to forſake willingly the loue of the
ſame vertue, which is with anxiety,
and ſuperfluous propriety, for the
deſire to haue the ſame vertue vvith
ſatisfaction, and be content to beare
the burthen of her imperfection a-
gainſt her will, to conforme her ſelfe
wholy vnto Gods will, is a moſt great
renunciation, and ſurpaſſeth all other
vertues. And here muſt be taken away
the anxiety, and griefe that we haue
to obtaine it: and note well, that the
more diligence we ſhall vſe with anxiety, and propriety, for to obtaine it
of God, the leſſe ſhall we haue it.

The third is the deſire of ſuffering,
againſt which although our nature re-
pugne, as a thing contrary to ſenſe : it
may happen neuertheleſſe, that the deſire to haue it, is too great by exceſſe of
anxiety, & ſelf loue in the ſame; as women with child are accuſtomed to exceed in appetits of duſt, coales, and the
like

like things difpleafing to taft. Moreouer to fuffer for the loue of God, is a
thing of this nature that giueth great
fatisfaction to the foule, for the excellency and highnes therof, and therefore may be an obiect of felf loue; but
that defire of fuffering is moft accep-
table to God, which is with the forefaid renunciation, and conformity.

Furthermore, they that afpire to
the height of perfection, are to be aduertifed, that it doth not confift (as
many thinke) alwaies to haue their
thoughts, & affections on a croffe, &
in the greateft afflictions that are: for
how great feruour foeuer they haue, in
the end nature wil feele it, & the mind
will be afflicted, and fuch fadneffe will
breed a continuall violence, and difficulty to work, in the which it feemeth
vnto them, there is great fanctity, and
merit, but certainely it is a great hinderance of the fame, feeing that euery
little thing becometh difficult to a fad
foule: and on the contrary cherefulnes affuuageth, and lightneth all labour hovv great foeuer it be.

It

It is not then the higheſt act of vertue , to deſire to ſuffer , & indure, for
this very ſuffering hath his limits, and
ought to be done in meaſure : but the
higheſt act is, a perfect contentment ,
that riſeth from a full, & entire conformity vvith the diuine Will , cauſing a
moſt prompt diſpoſition to ſubmit her
ſelfe in all,and by all , to that vvhich
God vvil vvork in her,by her, & vvith
her, according to his diuine pleaſure .
And for that this too great anxiety, to
deſire to ſuffer , and indure , taketh a-
vvay ſuch contentment, and hindreth
the perfection of operations; the ſoule
ought to take avvay , and cut off the
thoughts of croſſes,&paines,vvhē it is
not time to ſuffer,conuerting and chā-
ging all into this cherefulnes of conformity with God , to the vvhich, the
thinking of pleaſant and delightfull
things (ſo they be holy)helpeth much,
ſot that ſuch things are conformable
to perfection.

Of this cherefulnes ſpringeth a
promptnes to all operations, ſtrength
to ſurmount difficulties, and ioy of
hart

hart and vnderstanding, as the Apoftle faith: *Gaudete in Domino femper, ite-
rum dico gaudete*. Reioyce in our Lord
alwaies, againe I fay reioyce . Agility
to take in hand any good worke, facility to execute and end it, & fweetnes
in all things, euen in the croffe it felfe,
vvhen it is taken only for the loue
of God, & to pleafe him . And if vve
haue not fuch cheerfulnes, at the leaft
vve ought to defire it, and inforce our
felues to haue it in refifting all hinderances that the diuell fhall oppofe.

Our Lord vvas fingularly indued
vvith this alacrity, and fhevved it in
his countenance, rendering himfelfe
very amiable, vvherby is manifeft
that he thought not allvvaies on his
paffion, but that he diuerted and reti-
red his mind & thoughts, except vvhẽ
he knevv that it vvas the vvill of his
Father he fhould, and thought on ioyfull things vvith a pleafant afpect, and
vvith a fvveet and gratious countenance, accompanied vvith grauity
and vvords of vveight, to dravv the
hatts of the people vvith mildnes and
autho-

authority; & vvith this alacrity he in-
dured, and suffered aftervvards the
subtraction, or taking of it away in the
time of his passion.

THE FIFTH
Degree.

CHAP. VIII.

THE soule being in this conformity, tranquillity, and cheerfulnes vvhich hath byn said, vvith
progresse in perfect vertues, and vvith
great povver of the superiour part o-
uer the inferiour, by reason of the long
habit, and great facility she hath gotten in repressing, & subduing the motions of her passions; God is vvont
after this, or vvhen he thinketh good,
to permit her to begin to feele great
tentations, the like or greater then
those vvhich she suffered in the beginning of her conuersion, to vvit, of the
flesh, of impatience, of feare, of difficultyes, and other the like, in such
sort,

sort, that she beginneth againe to feele
a great rebellion in her inferiour part,
against the superiour , and the diuell
sharply tempteth her , in so much that
she is forced to returne to fight,& that
with great difficulty:but notwithstanding , the superiour part generously
fighteth , gaineth, and beareth avvay
the victory.

    This mutation and vnexpected
change resebleth the imperfect state ,
of a nouice or a beginner only . The
rebellions of the interiour part,against
the superiour, the representations of
diuells, the motions of sensuality , &
the newnes vnaccustomed , is as it
were against the commō stile of grace,
that happeneth to vs ordinarily after
the first assaultes of temptations , and
the victory ouer them , hauing gotten
the habits of perfect vertues , and
in such sort subdued sensuality , that
scarcely it did once kicke or re-
pugne: Al these things are accustomed
to put the soule in great perill, of thinking she goeth backward , and that
she hath giuen occasion of her being

in

in so euill an estate wherof is wont to
rise in her mind vnquietnes, despaire,
and great decay of wonted force, and
therfore it behoueth that she stād well
vpon her guard, and before all things
consider and obserue, that the will by
the grace of God is resolute, rather to
dye a thousand tymes, then to offend
God in the least thing that is. And for
that sinne consisteth in the will, she
ought also firmly to perswade her self,
that she is farre from committing of
it, seeing that all her griefe commeth
of that ; to witt, of those contrary
motions, her will being so earnestly
bent, not to offend God. And which
is more she ought to be secure that she
hath not on her part giuen occasions
to such tentatiōs, seing that she abhorreth, and detesteth them greatly : and
principally for that she desireth to cō-
forme her self altogeather to the diuine
vvill, and to disappropriate herselfe of
all thinges created. She must likewise
be aduertised that she doth performe
this vvhile diuers actes of vertue with
the superiour part, for so much as

hereby through diuine grace the fpirit is made more vigorous , although
the flefh be moued & incumbred with
no fmall perturbatiõs, & this fo much
the more , for that fhe fhall find mani-
feftly and affuredly , that there is no
offence therin : and if fhe find that fhe
cannot fufficiently refolue her felfe,for
her continuall feares , and remorie of
confcience, let her remit herfelf , and
repofe wholy on the iudgment of him,
that hath the guiding of her foule.

Moreouer fhe muft be aduertifed
that fuch temptations , although they
feeme vnto her to be the fame that fhe
was wont to endure in the beginning,
are notvvithftanding very much different , if fhe confider the caufe from
vvhence they proceed : for that then
the fuperiour part being deftitute of
good habits, vertues and graces that
giue great ftrength , and the inferiour
part full of euill habits , very ftrong &
ftubborn, together with the fraudulét
fleights of the diuell concurring therin, no meruaile that the flefh did fight
and rebell againft the fpirit, vntill fuch
time

tyme as the superiour part were made strong and vigorous: but then our Lord gaue strength to resist, and vanquish the inferiour part, which being thus tamed, the battaile ceaseth soone after, with a submission and tranquillity between the one & the other; our Lord permitting all this, to the end, that by the vvay of combat, to his imitation, we may obtaine the victory, and also by this meanes be made partakers of his celestiall gifts and vertues.

But when after all this the teptations teturne, the soule being already fortified, and not hauing giuen any occasion therunto, then she must assuredly know, that this is an expresse prouidence of God, who will haue it so, and that such temptations doe not take their beginning of the interiour, to wit, of any vice, or default that is in her, but come of other causes: and this great & secret instructiō helpeth much to know to what end our Lord worketh and permitteth all this. For first it is to the end, that the repose and

C 2   peace

peace that she had before, be not occasion to her of so great satisfaction,
and cotentmet that she come to delight
much in her self for it, & so be in danger to fall into pride . Secondly that
self-loue which subtilly vseth oftentymes to enter therin be quite extin-
guished . Thirdly that there may increase, and continue in the soule the
knowledg of her basnes & litle worth.
Fourthly that she may attaine to a new
light, and know that perfection doth
not consist in being free from temptations & in hauing peace betwene sensuality and reason : for it may so fall
out, that these temptations will be
more vehement, then those that she
had before, and that she shall suffer
much by them, and therfore she ought
to hold her selfe assured that our Lord
by such meanes will bring her to greater vertue .

Wherfore when she beginneth
to enter into such afflictions or troubles she ought before all things to hu-
ble her self and descend into her owne
nothing, & acknowledg herselfe worthy

thy of all temptations: & in the ſame
manner, as ſhe was already before
accuſtomed, to receyue with contentment the contempt and affliƈtions outwardly: ſo ought ſhe to inforce herſelfe
to reioyce in that our Lord is pleaſed
to humble her, & to permit her thus to
be buffeted of the diuell. Secondly ſhe
ought to be willing to want the peace
& repoſe that ſhe felt when ſhe had no
great temptations, and likwiſe all con-
tétment which ſhe had therin. And how
much the more ſuch repoſe is a high &
excellent good, ſo much the greater
ſacrifice it is, and more pleaſing vnto
God, to be willingly depriued therof
for the loue of him.

Thirdly, ſhe ought to admit
with the ſame affeƈtion, and promptnes, as is ſpoken of before, the ſub-
traƈtion or withdrawing that our Lord
doth vſe, which conſiſteth in this, that
he doth not permit the vertue or power of the ſuperiour part, to redound
and worke in the inferiour, by giuing
it ſuch force as that it ſhould not feele
theſe temptations: which would be,

C 3 if

if God did concurre therin as before:
but our Lord withdraweth such concourſe, & frō hence proceedeth anxiety and affliction. Fourthly ſhe ought
not to inforce herſelf to driue away
theſe temptations with great penance
and mortification of nature, as ſhe did
at the beginning whē ſhe was a Nouice
for by that way (as is read of ſome
Saints) the temptations increaſe rather then otherwiſe, but ſhe ought to
ſubmit her ſelfe vnto God with humility, for to ſuffer them willingly, as
long as it is in his will and pleaſure, &
then not to care for them, but to contemne them.

Afterwardes, of this followeth the
conformity to the diuine will greater
then euer, ſeeing that to conforme her
ſelfe vnto him, the ſoule is content to
be left comfortleſſe, and to ſuffer ſuch
paine & confuſion which is moſt pleaſing to his diuine maieſty: beſides that,
it is very conformable to that which
our Redeemer did, when being in the
gardē he would that the inferiour part
ſhould find difficulty to ſuffer, & neuer
the-

theleſſe he ſaid , *non mea, ſed tua volun-tas fiat*, not my will (o father)but thine be done. And of this conformity riſeth in the ſoule not only a loue of vnion that transformeth it into God more highly , but alſo a loue & deſire of the croſſe,in conformity with our Sauiour when as to accompliſh the diuine will, ſhe is cõtent to ſuffer temptation . And here ſhe doth not only offer, and de-dicate herſelfe vnto God, but doth alſo ſacrifice herſelfe vnto him .

THE SIXT
Degree .

CHAP. IX.

BEſide s all this that hath bene ſaid , the affliction and paine is accuſtomed to paſſe further , and come euen to the ſuperiour part where vertues and ſpirit make their reſidéce. And ſo ſhe ſhall perceaue her ſelfe to faile and want light in her vnderſtan-ding, and good purpoſes, and deſires

C 4   in

in her affections, promptnes to doe
well, ftrength and patience and the
like, in fuch fort, as where before fhe
did fight with great force and vigour,
now it will feeme vnto her, that fhe is
without ftrength and vertue, and that
fhe cannot refift, and euery litle ftraw
will feeme vnto her a block, and fo
fhall feele and perceaue nothing but
obfcurity, blindnes, great darknes,
aridity or drineffe, grief, tepidity, rebellion, pufillanimity, confufion and
great oppreffion, feeming vnto her vn-
poffible to returne to her firft defigne-
mentes and good purpofes. And here
in very truth is great danger, if fhe doe
not inforce herfelf to remedy it, as fhe
fhould, to the end fhe fall not into fũ-
dry great inconueniences, when fhe is
thus abandoned, which happeneth
in diuers manners.

First in apprehending too firmly
all this that hath bene fpoken of, to be
a great mifery, and for this caufe,
afflicting her felfe, and growing fad.
Secondly too earneft fetting her felfe
to thinke of what caufe they proceed,
                                    attri-

attributing all to her owne defaults,
and inforcing her ſelfe to looke curiouſly into them . Thirdly of ſet purpoſe , procuring with great diligence
to free herſelfe of them , to take order
to remedy all , and returne to her firſt
eſtate , eſteeming the preſent to be
miſerable, and yet neuertheleſſe lee-
ſing all this labour: for this being not
the true way , nor the remedy of her
euill,ſhe findeth the trouble to be therby increaſed . Fourthly for this cauſe,
the ſoule is accuſtomed to fall into impatience,feare, and puſillanimity and
in danger to deſpaire , it ſeeming vnto
her that nothing doth help her, and
that ſhe goeth from euill to worſe. Sup-
poſing then the ſoule to be exerciſed
in theſe foreſaid degrees, it is needfull
ſhe conſider with her ſelfe , and principally with the help of him that guideth
her,the ſecret & meruailous miſteries
that are hidden herin. For the firſt the,
let her know that the true cauſe of all
that is ſaid, is the diuine prouidence,
who willing to make proofe, and to
purify a ſoule , after he hath enriched
it

it with vertues, and great ſtrength in
the ſuperiour part, is wont to retire his
accuſtomed ſuccours, without the
which theſe vertues cannot worke:
wherof it cōmeth, that although ſhe
haue them, notwithſtanding they are
not of any force, and it ſeemeth to her
that ſhe hath them not: and from hēce
followeth, darknes, ariditie & other
miſeries already ſpoken of; notwithſtanding the graces and foreſaid vertues remaining in the ſoule as before.

For the ſecond, this ſubtraction,
or diuine withdrawing doth not proceed of the abſence of vertues, giftes,
and graces, ſeeing that they remayne
entirely in the ſoule, and it doth leſſe
proceed from the action of them, for
ſo much as indeed the ſoule is depriued therof. But we muſt conſider that
in internall and ſpirituall actions, there
is a direct act, that tendeth directly to
God, to wit, the ſame internall act or
operation touching his obiect: as for
example, the practicall knowledg and
election, or lawfull deſire, to haue a
wil to ſuffer, to haue a will to loue God,
to

to haue a will to be temperate, chaſt, obedient, not to conſẽt vnto ſinne &c. There is alſo the act reflectiue, that turneth towardes it ſelfe, to wit, to diſcerne and iudge whether he doth ſuch an act, wherby he may receaue contentment, and reioce therin for the glory of God, for that he diſcerneth himſelfe by the ſame to be ſtrong, & victorious ouer temptations, with great repoſe of the ſoule.

Of theſe two, the firſt is the pure act of vertue, the ſecond is the fruit that redoundeth in vs, and the fruitiõ of the ſame vertue, & this is moſt cleare that the act of temperance doth not conſiſt to perceaue that he hath it, or to reioyce in it, or content himſelfe therin, but to deſire it, and effectuate it. Now God concurreth in the firſt, & by that meanes the acts of vertue are performed, but he withdraweth the ſecond, to wit, our knowledge, reflection, iudgment, and ſatisfaction to haue done them, and therfore it ſeemeth to vs, that we do them not, & in the place of the knowledge with-

drawn, hapneth darknes & blindnes,
in place of the ioyful affectiō succedeth
aridity & drinesse: euen as it hapneth
to him, that is almost starued, who receiuing food into his stomake neither
feeleth nor tasteth it, it is cleare that he
eateth, & notwithstanding it seemeth
vnto him, he eateth not, & hath in a
māner no more satisfaction of such an
act, then if he had not done it. Seeing
thē that it is not properly vertue to
perceaue our interiour actions, & that
therin doth not cōsist vertuous effects
and operations, being only satisfactiō
vnto our selues, our Lord pretending
to bereaue vs of all our proper tast &
interest, as a hinderance betwixt him
and vs, leaueth vs the purity of vertue,
which is no other thing but to desire it,
and put it in effect, and taketh away
the second, which is a certaine selfe-
loue more subtile then those that haue
yet bene specified, & an interest with
the which the soule nourisheth it selfe,
and such as diuerteth vs from greater
vnion with God: and this being so, it
is plainly to be seene, that there is not
                                        only

only no euill herin , nor any danger to
be feared , but that the foule by fuch a
diuine work is purified the more in
vertue,and is purged from all proprieties , and felfe intereft , although it
be very hidden , and is rayfed to a degree , and difpofition of greater grace,
and much more vnion with God then
before . For to make all this manifeft,
the foule that is come to this eftate
muft be aduertifed of two pointes .
The firft , that if fhe will examine the
purity of vertue , fhe fhall fee the fame
in her actions more then euer fhe did.
For if one fhould demaund of her in
thefe griefes , obfcurities and rebellions , if fhe would offend God , fhe
would prefently anfwere , that fhe had
rather dye a thoufand deaths , then to
commit the leaft finne and imperfection. If any fhould afke her whether
fhe would conforme her felfe vnto the
diuine will , fhe would fay , that fhe
greatly defired it , and now more then
euer , in fuch fort , that fhe would willingly dy for Gods honour and glory.
The like would fhe fay if fhe were demanded

manded, whether she desired to better
her estate, to know her defaultes, to
amend her life, whether she desired the
hatred of her selfe, the loue of God &
of perfection; and finally concerning
the exteriour actes of vertue, she notwithstanding all the afflictions leaueth
not in tyme to accomplish with attention all that which she is accustomed,
and to giue her selfe to the entire ob-
seruance of her vocation, which is an
euident signe, that the pure vertue is
not one whit relented or diminished,
but is more excellent : although the
soule be destitute, and depriued of the
tast of vertue, which was wont to ayd
her. The second point is to discerne
the difference of such an estate, from
that in which the soule felt the like
griefes, and obscurities, in the beginning, but by her fault and negligence,
for so much as then she lost the actes of
vertue. and the desire of perfection ;
and if by chaunce she felt any, they
were wholly without operation and
efficacy and in that state the soule leaueth the great good that before she
had

had attained vnto, going from euill to
worfe, with danger of her ruine.

She ought alfo to marke the mar-
ueilous height of this eftate, befides
that which hath byn faid : firft becaufe
this is a liuely and excellent imitation
of our Lord and Sauiour Iefus Chrift,
of whom it is written in the beginning
of his dolorous paffion : *Cœpit pauere,
tædere, & mœftus effe;* that is to fay,
he began to be troubled, to feare, and
became fad : and after he faid, *Triftis
eft anima mea vfque ad mortem,* my
foule is forrowfull euen vnto death.
Now we muft confider three pointes.
Firft the greatnes of the paine and torments that he was prefently to endure. Secondly that then was vvith-
dravvne from him the concurrence of
ftrength, patience, magnanimity, & the
like vertues, concerning the feeling of
them in the manner aforefaid, and
for that caufe prefently fell into fo
great anguifh, feare, & heauines, that
the leaft of his forrowes feemed vnto
him infupportable, wherof before he
reioyced fo much in thinking of the,
faying

saying: *Baptismo habeo baptizari, & quomodo coarctor vsque dum perficiatur* :
I haue to be baptiſed with a Baptiſme,
& how am I ſtraitned vntill it be diſ-
patched. Thirdly that with all this, the
ſtedfaſtnes of vertue was moſt firme &
more ſtable then euer , ſeeing that in
theſe words to his Apoſtles *Surgite, ea-
mus*, ariſe let vs go (that is) to meet thē
that came to apprehend him , he diſcouered a meruailous promptnes to
ſuffer, patience, ſtrength, and a gene-
roſity of hart, not to be ouercome or
quailed by ſuch a withdrawing or
ſubtractiō before mētioned , by which
the holy Doctors ſay , that our Lord
merited then for the holy Martyrs &
other Saints , who in their torments
and paines were ſo richly armed with
patience, ſtrength, magnanimity & o-
ther vertues in the ſuperiour part, that
by the ſame vertues they did ſo tri-
umph & reioyce euen in the middeſt
of their paines & torments as we read
of many holy Martyrs . When then it
ſhall pleaſe our Lord to take away &
bereaue a ſoule, for the loue he beares
it,

it, of this garmēt with the foreſaid ſubtraction, or withdrawing, as he doth
in this eſtate, then it is cleare, that
he bringeth her to a higher imitation
of himſelfe, then was the other, ſeeing that the ſame ſubtraction vvas v-
ſed to him by his eternall Father.

And beſides this reaſon of the
moſt liuely imitatiō of our Lord there
followeth others alſo, to wit, that how
much the ſuperior part is more noble
then the inferiour, or then the body :
ſo much more the ſuffering of it, or
both together, is more noble then a-
ny martyrdome whatſoeuer of body
only, if it be without the other. And
moreouer to ſuffer with this fredom,
and liberty or ſenſible force of vertue,
with which the Martyrs vvere indued
was as eaſyly vnto them, as if they
had bene in the middeſt of roſes. But
with this ſubtraction or withdravv-
ing it ſeemeth not only difficult, but
alſo impoſſible. Soe that vvith al this
difficulty to be thus magnanimous,
and couragious with all efficacy, maketh vs more apt, and prepared for
higher

higher vertue, and greater merit.
And finally to find our selues so freely
and highly raysed vnto vertue, naturally it is an occasion of perill & danger of pride : wherfore vnto S. *Paul*
(*Ne magnitudo reuelationum extolle-
ret eum* , least the greatnes of his reuelations should extoll him) there vvas
giuen to preserue him the temptation
of the flesh, so to counterpoise the
daunger which might follow : by this
height of vertue the soule is plunged
into this extreme low estate , by the
feeling which she hath of troubles &
feares &c. And therfore she is secure,
that is, she is preserued from danger,
vvhich is a signe of higher estate, for
that she hath a great foundation of humility , and knowledg of her owne
basenes. This as it seemeth may be gathered of the temptation of *S. Paul* ,
which vvas giuen him for auoyding
the perill vvherin he vvas : vvherof it
follovveth , that the hauing of that
temptation of the flesh , was a higher
estate, then the first, seeing that by this
meanes the hinderances and imperfe-
                                    &ions

ctions of the first are taken avvay, and
he is made more secure therby, in
such sort , as this estate is a certaine
probation , that God maketh of his
elect, a liuely imitation of our Lord
and Sauiour Iesus Christ , a more excellent Martyrdome , then the exteriour, and founded vpon profound humility , which is more sure then any
other vvhatsoeuer , and is of greater
merit , and a disposition to receiue
greater gifts , and graces, and which
is more , an enemy to proper loue; for
that it taketh away the satisfaction and
contentment that is receaued of vertues , and so by consequence increaseth , and commeth to be of greater
conformity with the diuine will, & is
enkindled more in loue towards God,
then the others before mentioned :
seeeing that for to satisfy Almighty
God , a man depriueth himselfe of
so great a good , and remayneth with
the pure actes of vertues naked of all
sensible ornaments, and selfe contentment .

  That vvhich ought aftervvardes
          to

to be practifed, is: Firft for fo much as
the diuell is vvont to trouble the foule
vvith many thoughtes, as if all this
happened for fome great defautls,
that were in her (which afflicteth
her much) to deliuer her felfe from
this, fhe ought to repent herfelf of all
her defects, finnes, and occafions that
fhe may haue giuen in this cafe, but
in generall, vvithout any more thinking therof, and for the reft, to remit
herfelfe vvholy vnto her Superiour,
belieuing in all things his aduife, and
renouncing her ovvne iudgment, keeping her felfe in peace, and repofe
of confcience, fuppofing a maxime,
vvhich is greatly neceffary in this fixt
degree, to wit, that a man ought not
to iudge of himfelfe, nor of vvhat he
feeleth in himfelfe, feing that the fubtraction maketh that he can haue no
light, reflection, nor perfect iudgmet
of his actions; but he ought to content himfelfe, and reioyce in this darknes, and aridity, and ought to humble
and fubmit himfelf to the iudgement
of another, anihilating and acknovvledging

ledging himfelfe vvorthy of this, and
of much vvorfe, vnvvorthy of al light,
and in fuch bafenes he ought to glo-
rify God.

Although that the motiõs of impatience, and other the like naturall motions be great, and make the foule to
become fad and melancholy, without
feeling any comfort, or folace, yet
muft fhe know, and labour to trie by
experience, that the forfaid fubmiffion, with this alfo confifteth in refigning, & remitting her felf wholy vnto
God, euen as one that is fick, vvho
although he cry through the veheme͂-
cy of his paines, neuerthelefse in will,
is fubmitted entirely vnto God, and
is content to fuffer any thing.

As for feare and pufillanimity (befides that which naturally the feeleth,
vvhich is not euil of it felfe) fhe ought
not to admit any more, nor to confent vnto it, but ought to endeauour
her felf to performe acts of fubmiffion,
confidence in God, familiarity & the
like.

And doing all this that is aboue
faid,

said, and with the same, denying herself in all things, and conforming herselfe vnto God, not willing any thing, but vvhat he vvilleth, if she feele these troubles, and darknes to increase, she must not for all that be afflicted, for any thing whatsoeuer it be; but without any kind of murmuring, she must seeke to forget her euill, and ought to know that God is accustomed to doe this, that is to say, to withdravv all consolation and help in our temptations. Therfore she must the redouble her cōformity & thanksgiuing vnto God, and quiet herselfe, and repose with assurance that in the end God vvill not leaue her, nor permit that she be tempted aboue her strength, which heere doth not consist vvholy in resistance against them, or putting them away, seeing that is not so much in our power by reason of the subtraction: but in this, to suffer and support them; & this is more sure & perfect, then extasy.

O F

OF THE SECOND
Eſtate.

CHAP. X.

VV Ho vvould thinke, that
there ſhould be any thing
yet left in the ſoule which
ſhe might renounce, forſake & withdravv herſelfe from, beſides this that
hath bene ſaid, & eſpecially the ſoule
being brought to the only pure and
direct act of vertue, in the which it ſeemeth there is nothing but true vertue,
& alſo bereaued of all proper intereſt.
But if we conſider that ſuch an act although it be thus purged, is a pure
act of election, and of our vvill, the
vvhich vvith his actiue vertue impe-
ratiue, in reſpect of the other powers,
vvorketh and produceth the acts of
vertue; it cannot be denyed, but that
there is proper vvill, and intereſt therin, although much purged, and by
conſequence there is ſomyvhat yet to
forſake

forſake, and to be purged.

The ſoule then that is left without any other action but to doe in the manner aboue explicated, being ariued to the foreſaid ſixt degree, our Lord is accuſtomed to withdraw by little, and little the povver to doe ſuch actes, taking novv one, novv another vntill ſuch tyme, that indeed he taketh away all, except the povver to conforme her ſelfe vnto the diuine vvill. And by experience it is proued that ſomtymes the ſoule findeth her ſelfe ſo oppreſſed with griefes and afflictions, and aſſayled vvith ſo many diſtractions, and miſeries, that vvilling to enforce herſelfe, yet ſhe cannot performe any act, neyther of thankes giuing towards God, nor of fortitude, nor of patience, nor of any other vertue, no not ſo much as to will that which is agreeable vnto God. And ſhe muſt remaine in this ſufferance, pierced through invvardlie vvith a thouſand temptations: ſo that as the Martyrs could not defend théſelues, from their torments & woûds,

but

but receiuing them , conformed thē-
ſelues to the diuine vvill: euen ſo muſt
the ſoule doe in this caſe , in vvhom it
may be, there remayneth not any a-
ctiue force , but only the paſſiue, enduring all for the loue of God , and
remaining content with the ſame .

But which is more, he is accuſtomed alſo to take a vvay ſuch an act of
conforming herſelfe to the diuine will
in ſuch manner , that ſhe hath not any
ſenſible feeling to do it, & alſo leſſe can
ſhe execute it : and there remayneth
no other thing, but a paſſiue tranquillity; by which, as a lambe before the
ſhearer , ſhe remaineth quiet, and ſuffereth God to accompliſh vvhatſoeuer
he pleaſeth .

This is an entire and abſolute ſubtraction of the actiue povver of the
ſoule , to vvit, that God vvithdraweth
in ſuch ſort his diuine cōcurrence that
the ſoule cannot in the ſuperiour part,
hovv holy or raiſed ſoeuer ſhe be ,
make any actiue operations , but only can remaine peaceable , and quiet ,
enduring vvillingly that vvhich God

D   per

permitteth to happen vnto her .

To such a vvithdrawing the soule ought to be correspondent vvith anihilating and acknovvledging herselfe to be pure nothing , and full of infinit sinnes and therfore vnworthy to performe any action of vertue : and she ought to reioyce in such contempt , that God vvorketh in her , taking frō her the povver to lift her hart vp vnto him , vvith a free renunciation ; she ought to be contented to vvant vvholy the actiue , and all the acts of vertue; the vvhich hovv much more they vvere pure, so much greater is the gift that God imparteth therin. After this it often happeneth , that the troubles and afflictions vvillbe not only as before but much greater; for hauing lost the rampire and fortresse of the actes of vertue , and moreouer in the concupiscible and inferiour part , there vvilbe raised motions so vehement and disordered , that she neuer felt the like in her life , in such sort , as it will seeme vnto her, that she is euen in hell it selfe : and heere she

must

muſt not arme herſelfe vvith any o-
ther armour , then vvith ſubmiſſion
and paſſiue tranquillity in ſupporting
all to ſatisfy almighty God , vvho vvil
haue it ſo . And ſhe ought to knovv ,
that ſuch ſubmiſſion and tranquillity
giueth to the ſoule a very great
ſtrength , not aƈtiue but paſſiue , by
the vvhich he giueth and leaueth herſelfe to be as a prey vnto God ; and ſo
like a moſt patient lambe ſuffereth all,
in great debility & feeblenes . Of this
peace and tranquillity followeth a cōformity with the aƈtiue vvil, although
paſſiue , but vvithout cōpariſon greater then the foreſaid , and an inexpli-
cable deification, in an aƈt yet paſſiue,
not of oblation, nor of gift , dedication , or holocauſt, but much more excellent and more perfeƈt , as to giue
themſelues vvholy as it vveɾe a prey
vnto almighty God .

  In this eſtate ſhe muſt be aduerti-
ſed of ſome things of much importāce.
one is , that the interiour , and impe-
ratiue aƈtions of vertue are not loſt,
but are made more aƈtiue then euer ,

in such sort that a person hath strength
to vvorke and exercise the partes and
powers of her body and soule in spea-
king, thinking, and doing, all that
is conuenient to be done, according to her vocation, yea euen in
performing acts of temperance, patience &c. Also when she ought to
ayd and help her neighbour, it is
with the accustomed affability: for the
act of commaundment, and practice
resteth in the soule, to wit, to commaund and, to direct all her actions
of commaund or execution. For the
subtraction or vvithdrawing ought to
be vnderstood in the vnderstanding
and vvill, concerning the proper interiour acts of the vvill, intention,
fruition, election, reioycing, satisfaction, & the like, which indeed are taken avvay.

Another is, that it must not be vnderstood, that our Lord taketh avvay
the gifts, or habits, but the acts, not giuing his help & concurrence, notwithstanding he doth not so alvvaies: for
that often in this estate, he letteth the
soule

foule be free,and at liberty to vvorke,
but ſometymes he ſuſpendeth it , and
this is done without any certaine rule
and when he pleaſeth . Therfore the
foule ought to be vvholy reſigned , to
be depriued of all aſts or not,as much
and vvhen it ſhall pleaſe God , and to
be alvvaies ready to renounce them
vvith this admirable indifferency .
When the aſtiue is taken away in the
manner beforeſaid, then the ſoule remaineth in the paſſiue ſtate in tvvo
ſorts. Firſt for that with promptnes &
great tranquillity ſhe ſubmitteth herſelfe to all the affliſtions, and foreſaid
troubles, and miſeries, induring them
moſt vvillingly , although ſhe be
tranſpierced , and wounded by them,
for the great reſolution ſhe hath made
rather to ſuffer a thouſand deaths thē
to offend God , and for that ſhe ſuffereth ſo many euill motions : and alſo
for that ſhe cannot performe any aſt
of vertue , but only ſuffereth ſuch af-
fliſtion for the loue of God .

    Secondly the ſoule in ſuch eſtate
being retyred to the deepeſt part of

her hart, (vvhich the Myſticall Deuines call *Pax animæ*, the peace of the
foule) operation being vvithdrawne,
ſhe giueth and ſubmitteth herſelf with
great promptnes vnto God, who worketh vvithin vvith the paſsiue conſent
of her free vvill , much more higher
acts , then of thanks-giuing , loue, v-
nion vvith him , election , or any o-
ther vertue , without taſt , only admitting them , and cooperating vvith
all her hart, and affection, in ſuch ſort,
that as the vnderſtanding retyred frō
the ſenſe in extaſy cannot be attentiue with her naturall forces to actiue
vertues , as ſhe was before , but receiueth diuine light , that worketh moſt
high vnderſtāding & knowledg in her
(vvhich the myſticall Deuines call *pati
diuina*:) now if in the vnderſtanding
rayſed aboue her naturall forces , our
Lord vvorketh this , the ſame may be
done , much more in the will , when
renouncing wholy the actiue , ſhe for-
ſaketh the ſame, & then our Lord rai-
ſing it into an extaſy & a moſt vertuous practiſe , worketh in her entirely
what

what he pleafeth, and this *pati diuina*, which is an eftate much higher thē the forefaid, for that extafy of the vnderftanding is dangerous, and few attaine vnto it, full of infinite occafions, and fubieƈts of curiofity and propriety : but heere the will renounceth and humbleth herfelfe, and vvith a moft affured confidence fubmitteth herfelfe vnto God: and of fuch an extafy all are capable, and it is much higher and excellent then the other, rendring the foule moft agreable and pleafing vnto God.

OF THE THIRD
and laft Eftate.

CHAP. XI.

FINALLY our Lord is accuftomed to take avvay not only the aƈtiue but alfo the forefaid paffiue, the will remayning in all, and by all naked and impotent for any thing. It is true fhe doth not refift, or oppofe her felfe

to this , but she suffereth herselfe to be
bereaued of all . And for the vnderstanding of this last estate, which is the
highest of all the others , it must be
noted, that the vertue and force of the
liberty which the will hath, is so great,
that she can renounce wholy her will ,
and wholy her liberty, and indeed be-
reaueth herselfe of them , as if she neuer had them ; and she doth this freely
with her good will: and by such a renunciation the will is made as it were
no will; in the manner, that as *S . Pau-*
line made himselfe a slaue to deliuer
another slaue : euen so the soule hath
power to doe with her interiour, and
with her free will and liberty ,

Then our Lord taketh away the
actiue , and the passiue by subtraction,
and all acts whatsoeuer, as if she were
not at all : and she doth not resist this,
but with an entire exhibition of such
a renunciation , concurring therwith,
commeth to be no practicall will, to
wit , that all the operations that she
doth, or can doe concerning herselfe
she doth not will them, nor doth the as
                                      of

of herſelf: yet willing them neuertheleſſe with a will conformable to the
diuine will, in which ſort ſhe willeth &
worketh them; and therfore she doth
them as commaunded immediatly of
the diuine will, without bringing therin any concurrence of her owne, putting the will of God in the place of
hers .

So as a large and ſpacious Pallace
of the which one only is maiſter , whē
he is abſent, he leaueth ſome friend
of his, abſolute maiſter , and there is
done all, that was done before , but
only by the commaundment of the
friend , and not of the other : euen ſo
the will renouncing it ſelfe wholy ,
aſwell in the aƈtiue as in the paſſiue,
although pure, and holy, not willing
but what God willeth; and now not
willing indeed neither more nor leſſe
to haue this ſatisfaƈtion neither , as is
ſaid , she renounceth in all thinges , &
wholy the ſaid aƈtiue & paſſiue, being
reſolued not to work at all, as with her
will, notwithſtanding she doth all euē
as before, but as thinges willed and
D 5   ordeyned

ordeyned by God not of herfelfe, leauing entirely & imedintly to the good
pleafure of God, the commaundmēt
of her body, foule, actions, motions,
and feelinges, as if truely she had no
manner of vvill: and to this God cor-
refpondeth as is faid, vvith the vvith-
dravving of all acts: and if peraduen-
ture she leaueth or doth the like acts
of vertue as before, then she leaueth
and doth them, not according to her
proper will, but for fo much as she
feeth the will of God to be, that she
leaue, or doe them. Our Lord and
maifter himfelf made this fubtraction
and renunciation in the garden, when
he faid *non mea, fed tua voluntas fiat*:
my father, not my vvill be done, but
thine: to wit, my vvill would, as cō-
formable to thine, eternall father, fuffer croffe, and torments with great
purity and admirable fanctitie, but
I renounce all this: and concerning
fufferance, I defire and will it, not for
that my vvill (although moft holy)
vvilleth and defireth it, but only for
that thine vvould haue it fo : and I
renounce

renounce vvholy myne. And thus it
becometh not a free vvill, and therfore I fay, *non mea fed tua voluntas,* let
my vvill be no vvill, for to giue place
to thine. Here the anihilation, depri-
uation, and fubtraction shineth mer-
uailoufly, there being not only coformity herein, but fomwhat that is much
greater and higher, for that the will
with fuch a renunciation linketh and
tyeth herfelfe, diueth, & is as it were
drowned in God, and as a thing wholy loft in it felfe, remaineth in the will
of God, greatly deified, by being to-
tally the fame, and vnited vnto it, &
this is obtained by the true, and reall
practice aforefaid. Amen.

The end of this Difcourfe.

D 6   H E R E

HERE
FOLLOWETH
THE LADDER
of Perfection.

THE FIRST EXERCISE
of *Anihilation*.

The prayer preparatory accustomed, ought to be made before the Exercise.

IN the beginning vve must imagine, that euē as the wicked spirit re-presented to our Lord the world, with all the kingdomes & greatnes of the same, with a desire to haue deceaued him, if it had bene in his power: in the same manner he inforceth him-selfe, and seeketh as much as he can

to

to deceaue vs , as often as he repreſē-
teth and putteth before vs , any proper intereſt or cōmoditie of ours : and
as our Lord caſt him off , and van-
quiſhed him , in refuſing all things , &
not admitting any thing , ſo ought we
to ouercome him , and driue him away
by the meanes of a perfect anibilation
of will , and to pray vnto our Lord ,
by this his holy and entire renunciatiō
he will giue vs his grace to obtaine full
& entire victory ouer the deuill & ſin.

The firſt point .

MAN , & whatſoeuer is created
concerning their firſt origen ,
proceedeth of nothing , & of himſelfe
by a thouſand thouſand waies , to
wit , by infinite miſeries of ſoule and
body , to the which he is ſubiect ,
is ready , and tending to returne to
the ſame nothing , yf God by his
bounty did not conſerue him : and a
man ſinning is made worſe then nothing . By the meanes of this conſideration of this our firſt origen , and of
all

all thinges created , we muſt endeauour to eſteeme our ſelues, and all
thinges created as nothing , and not to
loue, deſire, ſeeke, or will any thing
for our ſelues : and thus we ſhall get
a perfect anihilation of will.

The ſecond point.

VV E muſt conſider , that
this true anihilation ma-
keth the ſoule to become a true por-
traict and reſemblance of the ſoueraigne greatnes of God , for that it taketh
away the hinderāces that are betwene
God and the ſoule; which is done by
not willing , or deſiring any thing : &
thus ſhe becometh a moſt faire , and
cleare mirrour or looking-glaſſe. For
euen as when we would , that a glaſſe
ſhould receyue in it ſelfe perfectly &
entirely the image and figure of ſome
obiect , it is needfull that ſo much the
further the one be ſet from the other ,
as the obiect is greater in it ſelfe; ſo the
greatnes of God being infinite , by the
meanes of this anihilation , the ſoule
not

not only taketh from it felfe all obfta-
cles that hindereth it from vniting it
felfe with God; but which is more, by
a great fubmiffion in her bafenes, and
a true knowledg of the infinite greatnes of God, fhe draweth herfelfe infinitely far from the fame, and by this
means cōmeth to be difpofed, & able
to receyue in her this infinit obieƈt of
God; & the fame Lord by the pleafure
he taketh, & infinit loue that he beareth to this foule, imprinteth & engra-
ueth prefently in her a true refemblāce
image, & portraiƈt of all his greatnes,
euen to the laft center of the fame.

This anihilation is of great
force to purge the foule of paffions,
taking away entirely all the obieƈts of
them, feeing that he that hath no will
to any thing for himfelfe, hath not
what to defire, loue, feare, or hate:
wherof commeth alfo that it purifieth
the foule, concerning the intention,
taking away all pretence of any created end whatfoeuer in all our aƈtions,
and maketh it truly capable to haue
no will to any other thing then to the
pure

pure glory of God in himfelfe, feeing fhe careth for nothing els; from whēce alfo proceedeth an entire and totall victory ouer all temptations, feeing that vnto him that defireth nothing, the deuill hath not any obiect to prefent; and if he doth, he is prefently reiected, and driuen away with this refolution of not defiring any thing, and by this meanes he is in all things vanquifhed and put to flight. The effects and principall fignes of this anihilation are thefe that follow.

The firft is, that the gifts and graces that our Lord communicateth to the foule, that is endued therwith, fhe receiueth them not, nor retayneth them in her felfe, for fo much as that which is nothing cannot receiue in it felfe any thing, but receaueth them in God, and referreth them vnto him from whome they proceed.

Secondly that fhe doth not appropriate them to herfelfe, nor reioyce in fuch graces in her felfe, neither is fhe troubled if they be taken from her, or that fhe happen to loofe them, but equally

qually, whether ſhe hauing them or
no, ſhe remaineth content in her nothing.

Thirdly ſhe maketh no accōpt of
this grace, but for ſo much as our
Lord wilbe ſerued by the meanes of
the ſame.

Fourthly, ſhe doth not eſteeme the
grace in it ſelfe, but for that by the
meanes of it, ſhe commeth to a greater
knowledg of the giuer, and eſteemeth
him the more.

Fiftly, ſhe doth not exalt herſelfe
for any gift or grace that ſhe can receaue, but alwaies keeping herſelfe
in her nothing, remaineth in the ſame
conceipt and opinion of her baſenes.

Sixtly, in the works that ſhe doth,
ſhe knoweth truly that of herſelfe ſhe
doth nothing, but diſcouereth in a
high manner the diuine aſſiſtance in
thē, & that it is he which worketh all,
& whatſoeuer happeneth vnto her, although neuer ſo grieuous and hard to
ſupport, yet with an entire peace ſhe
repoſeth in him.

Seauenthly, in the tyme of ſub-
tra-

traction, & drinesse of spirit, she is not
moued with it, neither seeketh any
remedy, or consolation, but with
all submission imbraceth it, and giueth herselfe in prey vnto it; as vnto
a proper obiect of her nothing.

THE
EXERCISE
of Disappropriation.

The Prayer preparatory acoustomed.

 I R S T we must con-
sider how truly was ve-
rified in our Lord Ie-
sus Christ, that which
he said of himselfe: *vul-
pes foueas habent, & vo-
lucres cæli nidos : filius autem hominis
non habet vbi caput suum reclinet* ; that
is to say : the foxes haue dennes, and
the birds of the ayre their nests : but
the sonne of the virgin hath not where
to repose his head ; and how much are
we obliged to seeke with all our power

wer, to imitate him in difappropria-
ting our felues of all things , for to
anfwere the infinite loue he beareth
vnto vs. Secondly we muft pray vnto
our Lord with great feruour that he
would impart vnto vs this grace : and
we muft make a firme and conftant
refolution to be willing to accept it
with all our hart and affection, and to
difpofe our felues perfectly and wholy to the exercife and execution of al
that it requireth of vs .

The firft point.

VV E muft confider, that this
difappropriation is a refolute will , that commeth
from God , to be willing to be entirely depriued, concerning our affection,
and, as much as poffibly is conuenient
in effect alfo, of all that we haue , and
this becaufe there redoundeth thereby
greater glory vnto God . And by this
is vnderftood that we muft depriue
& difappropriate our felues, not only
of all created things, in as much as
they

they nourish, and intertaine in vs felf-
loue, and all other faultes, and imperfections that may be found in vs :
but which is more , we muft alfo depriue our felues of that which tou-
cheth vs nearer ,euen of vertues , and
graces that we receaue of God , of all
fatisfaction,contentment,confolation,
and of any other good , that by the
meanes of them , we may attribute to
our felues, refigning all this truly
vnto God , not defiring in thē , nor in
any liuing thing , other taft and contentment , then that his holy will be
entirely & fully accomplifhed in vs
& all perfons . And in the end being
depriued of all proper intereft, & the
vertues, and celeftiall graces remayning in vs , euen in their purity , and
perfection , we then ought to acknowledge our felues moft vnworthy
of them:and the more perfect they be,
fo much the more do they belong vnto our Lord . And therefore with an
entire , and perfect refignation vve
ought moft freely to offer them vnto
him in this their naturall purity, fim-
plicity

plicity & perfection , remitting them
vnto their firſt origen . And moreouer we muſt be alwaies prepared to
depriue our ſelues of all giftes , graces, and vertues , as if it were to giue,
and make a preſent of them , vnto any
creaturewhoſoeuer,as it ſhal pleaſe our
Lord to ordayne , & this for his loue,
and for his greater glory and honour.

The ſecond point .

THIS perfect diſappropriation
or renunciation , is a dependance , and participation of the
diuine , which is infinitly proper to
God , if we may ſo ſay : and neuertheleſſe concerning the affectiõ, our Lord
depriueth himſelfe, with a meruailous
great and excellent perfection , of all
that he hath,with peace , tranquillity ,
repoſe of ſpirit , and infinit magnanimity . This we ſee in God the Father,
who really communicateth himſelfe
to the Sonne , and Holy Ghoſt : and
which is more in effect, he communicateth his gifts vnto vs in creation , cõ-
ſerua-

ſeruation of his graces, as he doth impart them to all his Creatures, and in
permitting ſinnes. And in the work of
the incarnation, and in all other my-
ſteries of our redemption, we ſee how
he debaſeth himſelfe in thinges moſt
baſe, diſappropriating and depriuing
himſelfe of the contrary perfections.
And then when ſo many Angels departed from him, and ſo many ſoules
yet doe the ſame, incurring eternall
damnation, he depriueth himſelfe of
them, and of ſo many graces which
he hath imparted to them: we ſee
in him the ſame diſappropriation alſo in infinite other manners which
cannot be explicated. Of this may be
gathered, that this is a moſt high perfection to imitate God himſelfe in the
foreſaid manner by the means of ſuch
a diſappropriation.

　　The principall effects that this diſappropriation worketh, & produceth
in the ſoule, are theſe that follow.

　　Firſt, that the gifts that ſhe recey-
ueth of God, ſhe receaueth and vſeth
them, as if ſhe had not receaued them,
　　　　　　　　　　　　　　　　not

not putting any affection in them, but
offering the loue vvhich ſhe might
haue to them, and the gifts of God thē-
ſelues to him frō whom they proceed.

Secondly, that ſhe reioyceth in
the gifts that ſhe ſeeth in another,
although ſhe hath them not herſelfe,
as if they were her owne.

Thirdly, it maketh her ready and
prompt to depriue herſelfe of the graces and gifts which ſhe hath receaued,
to enrich her neighbour therwith,
and ſhe reioyceth much in this.

Fourthly, when ſhe findeth herſelfe depriued of all gifts aſwell ſpirituall, as corporal, and of all graces
in what manner ſoeuer, ſhe remayneth alſo content, as if ſhe had not
receaued them, and is not troubled,
nor diſquietted any thing at all. She
knoweth well all her neceſſities, and
miſeries, but neuertheles ſhe contenteth herſelfe in them, knowing truly
that ſhe hath nothing of herſelfe, and
that nothing appertayneth vnto her
being vnworthy of any thing.

THE

THE
EXERCISE
of Indifferency .

*The Prayer preparatory
as accustomed*

IRST we must profoundly think of the sense of these wordes *Sedere ad dexteram meam & sinistram, non est meũ dare vobis , sed quibus paratum est à Patre meo* : that is to say: To sit at my right hand, & left, is not myne to giue you, but to whom it is prepared of my Father . And how much more in reason are we obliged to be in all thinges subiect, and to remit our selues wholy to the good pleasure of God by the meanes of a perfect and totall indifferency ?

We must demaund humbly this grace of our Lord , with firme resolution, willingly to accept of it, and to

put

put in execution the diuine infpira-
tions, by which we may be conducted
and guided to the fame.

The firft point.

FIRST, confider that this indifferency is a moft excellent, diuine, &
high perfection, for that although
our Lord be of nature , and of will
moft refolute to all that he will doe,
and to all that which he doth , neuertheleffe concerning his affection, he is
wholy prepared , to doe or not to doe
any work whatfoeuer , if it were fo
conuenient for him , and if he had, or
might haue any fuperiour of whom he
depended; and mo reouer concerning
the effect , we fee that he doth put in
execution this diuine indifferency in
communicating his giftes vnto all
creatures, although different amongft
themfelues , as is feene in perfons of
diuerfities of vvills and humors , according as is written: *Pluit fuper iustos
& iniuftos* , that is to fay , he maketh
it to rayne vpon the iuft and vniuft, in
E   gi-

giuing ſomtymes as much grace to a
ſoule that hath committed many ſinns
in her life tyme , as he doth to another
who hath not committed ſo many ,
bringing them both to equall glory ,
not ceaſing to loue her, to moue her
vnto good, and to impart nevv graces
dayly vnto her , therby to draw her
vnto himſelf, & by infinit other waies ,
although ſuch a ſoule by reaſon of her
ingratitude is vnvvorthy of ſuch graces as our Lord worketh in her.

The ſecond point.

VVE muſt conſider that this
indifferency in vs , is a dependance , and participa-
tion of the forſaid , by the meanes
wherof we are prepared to receiue frō
the hand of God all things , although
neuer ſo contrary in themſelues , for
to accompliſh the will of God, in what
manner ſo euer it be , and euen then,
when he withdraweth from vs all the
graces, which vve perceaued we had
before, and all things that might bring
vs

vs any contentment, and ſatisfaction.
The effects and fruites of this indifferency are theſe that follow. Firſt, that
the ſoule endued herewith, addreſſeth
the eyes of her ſpirit to conſider attentiuely, and in very deed is attentiue to
execute all whatſoeuer God vvill doe
with her.

Secōdly, this indifferēcy cauſeth one
to haue a great & magnanimous cou-
rage, by it they are diſpoſed, and are
made prōpt, & prepared to al things:
& of this ſpringeth a ſincerity of hart,
that maketh the loue of God to increaſe in the ſoule.

Thirdly the ſoule that is indifferēt,
accepteth, and withall her forces con-
ſenteth to all that God vvill vvorke in
her, and vvith great promptnes putteth it in execution, although it ſeeme
vnto her troubleſome, ſharp, grieuous, and vneaſy to ſupport, repug-
nant to her will, contrary to her inclination, and her proper iudgment or
of vvhat ſort ſoeuer it be : in vvhich
oftentymes many ſoules doe faile e-
uen of ſpirituall perſons, vvho for wāt

of this indifferency, and deceaued by
selfe loue, doe hinder oftentimes that
vvhich God vvould vvorke in them.

Fourthly, it maketh the soule prepared to liue, or die, to receaue consolation, or affliction, and to take all
thinges in good part, that can happen
either to herselfe, or others, and also
the vniuersall miseries vvhich our
Lord permitteth to happen in his
Church. Briefly she receaueth all
thinges equally, and in one manner,
from the hand of God.

Fiftly, vvhat thing soeuer she hath
she setteth not her affection thereon,
how good, or spirituall soeuer it be,
in vvhich many soules willingly stum-
ble, proposing vnto themselues in
their actions, a good intention truly
in it selfe, but according to their fa-
shion, and make great accompt of
certaine exercises that they doe, and
vvhich they much esteeme. But the
the soule indifferent, setting all things
aside, harkneth, considereth, and stu-
dieth with great diligence how to follow and put in execution the pure, &
true

true interiour motions of grace, and diuine inſpirations, and to doe what-ſoeuer ſhe knoweth may redound to the greateſt honour and glory of God.

Sixtly in tyme of conſolation, ſhe doth not purpoſe to do difficult mat-ters, and of great perfection, neither doth ſhe ſuffer her ſelf to be tranſpor-ted by the exceſſiue guſt, & ſvveetnes that ſhe feeleth therin; but all that ſhe purpoſeth to do, is done with repoſe, & maturity, alvvaies conditionally, according to the vvill of God, to the end that afterwards in the tyme of de-ſolation, ſhe remaine firme, ſtable, & conſtant in the ſame good purpoſes.

Seauenthly, in great ſolemnities, & like occaſions ſhe doth not conſider, nor rely vpõ her ovvne induſtry, nei-ther doth ſhe make too long prepara-tions: but vſing in this conuenient di-ligence, dependeth wholy, and with great ſimplicity on God, ſuffering herſelfe to be gouerned by him, as he beſt pleaſeth.

E 3   THE

THE FOVRTH
EXERCISE
of Conformity.

*The Prayer preparatory in the man-
ner accustomed.*

IRST we must con-
sider in these wordes
*(Cibus meus est, vt faci-
am voluntatem Patris
mei qui in cælis est)*
that is to say , my meat
is to doe the will of my father vvhich
is in heauen : and in other like spea-
ches the great conformity that our Sauiour Iesus had with the will of his e-
ternall father , so that in all his workes
he protested that he pretended no o-
ther thing, but entirely to put the same
in execution. And of this we may gather how much more vve are obliged
to do the same in his imitation , inforcing our selues as much as shalbe possible ; and with the greatest affection to
bend

bend & submit our will to be conformable vnto Gods, and to conceaue an
earneſt and vehement deſire therof,
which ought to moue vs humbly to
beſeech the diuine maieſty, that in the
vertue of the merits of his deare Sône,
our Lord Ieſus Chriſt, and by the
ſame conformity aforeſaid that was in
him, he vvould vouchſafe to impart
vs aboundantly this grace.

The firſt point.

VVE muſt conſider, that this
conformity is no other
thing then a totall and re-
ſolute dependance and ſubiection of
our will to the deuine in al our works,
occurrences, chaunces, vvhatſoeuer
they be: and moreouer that all things
whatſoeuer they are, are neither good
nor holy, but in as much as they are
beautified & ſanctified vvith the vvill
of God; and although they be indifferent, yea and ſeeme ſomtimes impertinent and not to the purpoſe in as
much, notwithſtanding as they pro-

E 4   ceed

ceed, and depend of the vvill of God,
they are very good, and tend to a very good end, and to the glory of God;
and therfore we ought to vveigh wel,
and attentiuely to confider, how high
and perfect a thing it is to be thus cō-
formed to vvhatfoeuer vve find to be
Gods will, in all things & at all tymes;
and how much the endeauouring, &
practifing of it importeth, and hovv
neceffary it is, if we defire to attayne
to great perfection.

The fecond point.

CONSIDER that this is a moſt
high perfection of God himſelfe
and which we fee to ſhine in the
diuine attributes; which in their workes, and in themſelues are infinitly
conformable to the will of God, and
from hence ſpringeth this vnſpeakable
harmony in them, as is ſeene meruailouſly alſo in the diuine perſons in
all exteriour and interiour actions, aſwell in that concerning created things
as in all increated acts of knowledg,
loue

loue , enioying , ioy , and infinit o-
thers . This conformity is ſeene alſo
amongſt the bleſſed ſpirits and ſoules
in heauen, who at the leaſt ſigne they
perceaue of the will of God , are al-
waves prepared to obey it , and obey
it with great promptnes: it is alſo ſeene
in all created thinges, and euen in inſē-
ſible creatures , as is read in the Goſpel,
quia mare & venti obediunt ei , for that
the ſea , and the winds obey him ; but
aboue all thinges it is moſt apparent in
the ſacred humanity of our Lord Ieſus
Chriſt with the ſecond Perſon of the
Trinity (to whom it is vnited) and
with his eternall Father, & in the inferiour part, with the ſuperiour in all his
powers, affections, and operations: &
likewiſe it is ſeene truly and perfectly
in the naturall repugnance that he felt
in conſideration of the torments, pains,
and exceſſiue dolours that he was to
ſuffer and how much the more he did
really & ſharply feele them , ſo much
the more he conformed himſelfe with
an vnſpeakable repoſe to the will of
his Father , in deſiring them ; ſo much

E 5   the

the more increased in him the repugnance, and sensibility of the griefes, in such sort, that the contentment in this conformity, did not bring him any assuagement of his sorrowes, but only made that his will sweetly reposed in them, and with so prompt and ready mind, he willed and desired them, that if the Iewes had not crucified him, he himselfe(if such had bene the will of his Father) was prepared to haue done it. We see also the like conformity in his most holy mother; which next vnto this of ourLord Iesus Chrift, was aboue all things created most singular and most perfect. And we must consider that all the forefaid conformities are represented in the diuine essence, which conteyneth in it selfe all things, and shineth infinitly in them, and in a manner that cannot be explicated, from which proceedeth great honour and glory vnto God.

THE

THE EFFECTS OF
*this conformity in a foule endued
therwith, are thefe that follow.*

FIRST it caufeth that the faid foule
ftudieth & laboureth with great
affection, and diligence to vnderftand and know in all thinges what is
the will of God, and to put it prompt-
ly and readily in execution, and not
to care for any other thing.

2. She findeth in all thinges repofe, & tranquillity, for the affurance
fhe hath, that in all thinges the will
of God is accomplifhed.

3. She enioyeth great liberty of
fpirit, free from all fcruples, vnquietnes and inward bitternes, faying often
vnto our Lord, thou knoweft Lord
that I defire no other thing, but the
accomplifhing of thy holy will,
make me to know it I befeech thee.

4. She acceptheth, and receaueth
afflictions, and tribulations as prefents
fent imediatly from the hand of God,

E 6   attri-

attributing them to no other cause.

5. She is not troubled for them, neither doth she lamēt, nor complaine vnto God, but to the imitation of our Lord Iesus Chriſt, ſaith, *non mea ſed tua voluntas fiat;* not myne but thy will be done.

6. She taketh pleaſure, & reioyceth in them: and the greater they are, and more contrary vnto her, ſhe maketh her cōmodity the more by them, by a greater knowledg of God, and a perfect ſubmiſſion vnto his diuine will.

7 When ſhe is calumniated, and perſecuted without any fault of her owne part, or any occaſion giuen, ſhe doth not ſeeke to iuſtify & excuſe herſelf but leaueth al entirely in the hands of God, for to ordayne the whole as he ſhall pleaſe.

8. Yf by wearines, and labour ſhe feele ſome vnquietnes, yet ſhe finds repoſe, conſidering that this is the will of God, conforming herſelfe vnto the ſame, without ſeeking in this any particuler intereſt, or good vnto herſelfe

THE

THE FIFTH
EXERCISE
of Vniformity.

The Prayer preparatory is to be made
as accuftomed.

IRST to confider in
thefe wordes, *Pater mi,*
non mea fed tua volūtas
*fiat:*Father, not my wil,
but thy will be done,
the great vnion that the
Sōne of God had with the will of God
his Father in a matter fo difficult, cō-
trary, and grieuous to nature, and fo
vnbefeeming (as may be thought) his
greatnes, as his paſſion was; and of this
we muſt gather, by how much greater
reafon we are obliged to doe the like,
in the imitation of fo rare an example
of our Lord Iefus Chriſt.

Secondly vve muſt with an extreme

treme defire feeke to obtaine this grace
and inftantly to pray vnto the eternall
father , that he will make vs worthy of it , by the merits of his deare
Sonne.

The firft point.

VVE muft confider that this
vniformity , befides that
which is contayned in the
conformity , doth more vnite the will,
with that of Gods. This taketh frõ vs
all repugnance , & difficulty , for that
in all things we not only will, what
our Lord willeth , but moreouer we
are incited , and moued to will it, only
for the reafon that God will haue it fo,
and all our contentment is to fatisfie
the diuine will , for the great vnion
that we haue with it : and this for the
loue of it felfe , and not for any other
refpect. And the fame loue inciteth vs
to the fame vnion with our euen Chriftian ; according to that which is writẽ
in the Acts of the Apoftles: *Erat credẽ-*
tium in Domino cor vnum,& anima vna,
all

al the faithful of our Lord had one hart
& one foule in the primitiue Church.
This vniformity fhineth , & is plainly
feene, firft in thinges wanting life , the
which by an inftinct of nature in fo
great diuerfities of operations agree
altogeather to execute meruailoufly
vvhatfoeuer they are ordeyned for by
God; & altogether accōplifh vniform-
ly this moft beautifull, moft excellent
and meruailous order , and harmony
of this vvorld , as vve fee for example in a houfe vvell ordered ,that many
feruāts performing duly diuers offices
that are commaunded them by their
maifter, come finally to accomplifh ,
and finifh all ,as one only affaire . But
this vniformity fhineth much more
perfectly in heauen amōgft the happy
fpirits , and foules ,in vvhom by the
efficacy of loue , the diuine will caufeth one hart, fpirit, and will,as if truly
altogether were but one,by a moft fin-
gular vnion with the fupreme will :
but aboue all it fhineth moft highly
and meruailoufly in the diuine attributes that agree , and accord in the
effence

essence, and diuine will, in the diuine
persons, and in the actes that they
produce.

THE EFFECTES
of this Vniformity in a soule
are these that
follow.

THE First is, that the soule that
is endued vvith this vniformity, not only contenteth herselfe in all that which is Gods will,
but moreouer vniteth herselfe with
the same will of God, and by this being made one selfe same thing with
it, she reioyceth equally in all things,
only for no other cause, but for that
the diuine will is pleased therwith,
and will haue it so.

2. In all places, and in all thinges
she findeth God, and vniteth herselfe
with him, and all creatures serue her
as a ladder to raise her vnto God.

3. For the sinnes she falleth into,
she is grieued for the offence that is
against

againſt Almighty God : but euen of
them alſo ſhe taketh occaſion to abaſe
herſelfe , and that with ſo much greater ſubmiſſion , penetrating into the
conſideration of the loue with the
which God hath permitted them , ſhe
vniteth herſelf vnto him .

4. How much the more it ſeemeth
to her ſomtymes that ſhe is depriued
of all grace , abandoned of God , and
left as ouerwhelmed in her miſeries;
ſo much the more , by the meanes of
them , ſhe vniteth herſelfe with God ,
knowing well , that the graces , that
ſhe firſt felt in aboundance are retyred
into God , and that they are kept, and
preſerued more ſecurely in him , then
when ſhe felt them in her ſelfe , and
is contented , and more reioyceth to
ſee them in God , then in herſelfe ,
and therefore rayſing and vniting
herſelfe with God, goeth to find them
in him , as in their proper origen and
conuenient place.

5. Being afflicted with any temptation either of the diuell , or other
creature whatſoeuer , ſhe reiecth , &

reſi-

refifteth all the euill that might happen vnto her by it, & withall acknowledging fuch creatures to be minifters
of God , who permitteth them for his
greater glory, euen by the meanes of
thefe temptations fhe commeth to v-
nite herfelfe vvith God.

6. How much the more fhe feeleth
herfelf fauoured of God by imparting
his celeftiall graces , and how much
the more excellent , and of greater cō-
fequence they are , fhe comming afterwardes to leaue them for to vnite
herfelfe more fully and perfectly vnto
God , from whom thefe forfaid graces proceed : fo much the more fhe
fheweth that fhe made much leffe e-
fteem of the giftes then of the giuer.

7. In all her interiour and exteriour operatiōs in a moment & twink-
ling of an eye , fhe vniteth her with
God , to know in them his will , & to
put it prefently in execution : and by
this all her actions are done vvithout
any difordinate affection , propriety ,
or particuler refpect.

THE

THE SIXT

EXERCISE

of Deiformity.

The preparatory Prayer accustomed before the Exercise.

N the beginning, and in consideratiõ of these wordes of our Lord, *Ego dixi Dij estis* : I haue said you are Gods &c. and in this that he said vnto his father, *vt vnum sint, sicut tu Pater in me, & ego in te, vt & ipse in nobis vnum sint*, that all may be one, as thou my Father art in me, & I in thee, so also that they may be one in vs. Here we must indeauour to penetrate into the excellency, and greatnes of the perfection vve are called vnto by our Lord Iesus, to vvit to vnite our selues in such sort by efficacy of wil

and

and by the vehemency of a louing affection to the diuine vvill : that being
transformed into the fame, vve be no
more, as we may fay, our felues, nor
that vvhich vve were before, but like
vnto God, and in God himfelfe, deified to the imitation of the vnion of the
Sonne of God, vvith his eternall Father.

2.   Being proftrate, with a moft
profound fubmiffion in the depth of
our nothing, in the prefence of the
height of his greatnes, as altogeather
aftonifhed, and relying on the loue
which incited him fo much to abafe
himfelfe, euen vnto vs, therby to
raife vs vp to himfelfe, vve muft
craue of this loue a correfpondence of
affection, which may liue in vs vvith
a vehement defire of this true and
perfect Deiformity in him.

The

The firft point.

VVE muft confider, that this Deiformity confifteth to haue our vvill vnited by fuch efficacy of loue vvith the diuine, that fhe feele no more from henceforward herfelfe, as if verily fhe were not at all, but that only fhe feele, in her the diuine vvill, & that all her actions, defires, & workes tend to the only accōplifhing of the fame. In fuch fort, that euen in vertues, and holy thinges, fhe vvilleth them no more, with a created vvill, nor by it, but only by the increated, made hers by an entire trāformation into it, confidering that our Lord Iefus intended to fhew this in thefe words, *non mea, fed tua voluntas fiat.*

The fecond point.

THAT this Deiformity is a dependance, and participation of the Deiformity in the diuine perfons, not only in their vnion, in the

the deuine essence, but also in the vnion, or rather vnity of will, vvhich is
betwene them, by the vertue of mutuall, and consubstantiall loue, which
is so great, that it interlaceth the deuine persons in the most pure essence
of the center of the diuinity, in such
sort, that although the persons be really distinct, they neuertheles transforme themselues by the force of this
loue so inwardly the one into the o-
ther, that one seemeth truly to be
the other, and principally in the center of the diuinity : and the like is
found in the diuine proprieties and
attributes, which although they are
perfectly vnited in the diuine sim-
plicity, they haue notvvithstanding
euery one his owne proper forme or
condition (the Deuines call it *rationem
formalem*, a formall reason:) but by an
ouerflowing or rather a kind of svval-
lowing & efficacy of loue, they come
to be so interlaced, and vnited in the
center of the diuinity, that it seemeth
they are all but one attribute in this
center of purity.

The

The third point.

THAT by a dependance, and by the reason of such a Deiformity she draweth by the same efficacy of loue, all created things to this soueraigne loue, as to their center, & origen from whence they are produced, and from thence to the foresaid most pure being, where they are ineffably deified.

The fourth point.

THAT the humanity of our Sauiour Iesus Christ, and of his most holy mother, and of all the blessed, by the working of God in them, and by the knowledg, and enioying that they haue of the diuinity, are as it vvere svvallovved vp and raised into this foresaid being, and vnity, and in the same most perfectly deified: & finally that all the Saints, and the iust yet vpon the earth, are transformed into God, and from thence afterwards

re-

turne to their being, as a drop of wa-
rer being caſt into a great veſſell full of
wyne, is changed into the ſame, and
after being out of the ſaid veſſell returneth to his firſt being.

The fifth point.

WE muſt conſider, that after the ſoule is arriued vnto ſuch an eſtate, that ſhe
hath taken away by the vertue of this
Deifying loue, and of the other foreſaid lights, all that might hinder the
working of God in her, then hath ſhe
attayned vnto this Deiformity; & this
Deiformity produceth theſe effects
that follow.

 1. She is Deiformed in all her a-
ctiōs, doing them, as if God did them,
and not herſelfe, and thus in them, &
by them entreth wholy vnto God,
and acknowledgeth him and enioyeth
him.

 2. Euen as a ſinner doth no actiō
but out of God, being depriued of his
grace, euen ſo on the contrary, ſuch a
ſoule

ſoule doth not find, or do any thing in which God is not , and by meanes wherof, ſhe doth not enter , & vnite herſelfe vnto God.

3 . She eſteemeth not of any thing, but in as much as it cōmeth from God or that it be done for God, & in God.

4 . Although that ſomtymes our Lord hide , and withdraw himſelfe from ſuch a ſoule, yet in this ſubtraction, and hiding , ſhe retireth wholy into God, hiding herſelfe in him, without any ſwetnes or feeling : yea hovv much the more, that by meanes of this rigour, leauing, ſharpnes, and bitternes, it ſeemeth that ſhe is far frō God: ſo much the more ſhe returneth, is Deiformed, and repoſeth in him.

5 . Being moſt certaine and aſſured , that ſhe herſelfe, as of herſelfe cānot performe any thing that is good, by reaſō of her totall vnability, knowing truly that ſhe is nothing, hath nothing, and can doe nothing of herſelfe, ſhe is not confounded, nor any whit troubled , yea euen in the middeſt of confuſions, ſhe findeth herſelfe much

F   aſſured,

affured, and contented , knowing certainly that fhe feeketh not any thing
proper , and that nothing of hers is
therin , but God doth all imediatly.

6 . Although fhe fhould raife the
dead,and do fuch meruailous workes,
& great things , yet fhe would neither
care, nor efteeme of fuch workes, or
be moued with them , but in as much
as God would,fhe fhould, & although
fhe fhould poffeffe all the treafures of
heauen and earth , fhe would not e-
fteeme of them in themfelues , nor for
herfelfe , but refer , and offer vp all
thinges vnto their firft origen from
whence they proceeded .

7 . Although fhe knew fenfibly that
fhe had God in her , yea and though
it were in the fame manner as our bleffed Lady his holy Mother had , fhe
would not be moued any more , then
if fhe did not perceaue any fuch thing
at all , or that fhe had him not in herfelfe, but in God only imitating herin
the glorious virgin Mary, who hauing
in her armes our bleffed Lord , held
him , as if fhe had not had him , but

as if her armes had bene Gods, & as
though he held himſelfe, & this was
the moſt excellent Deiformity of this
moſt pure ſoule.

8. When the ſoule that is come to
this Deiformity, ſeeth herſelfe to be
prayſed, ſhe taketh no maner of pleaſure therin, neither is ſhe troubled,
afflicted, altered, or moued any whit
at all, for ſo much as ſhe is vvholy in
God, and recevuing the praiſes that
belongeth to God, referreth and offereth them all vnto him.

9. Two ſoules Deiformed, hauing
betwene them great conformity of affectiō, intertayning one another with
mutuall loue of very great efficacy,
and with great diſapropriation and
therfore being to be ſeparated one
from the other, neuer ſo farr, for the
greater glory of God, careth nothing
at all, nor is any thing diſquieted, for
vvhatſoeuer accident hovv great or
grieuous that may befall her.

10. If God vvould publiſh to the
world the Deiformity that he hath giuen her, ſhe would not be diſquieted

or troubled, but would fay, Lord thou haft done it, doe whatfoeuer it pleafeth thee, for the whole work is thine.

OF SELFE-LOVE

THERE are three fortes of felfloue; the firft is in a worldly perfon, who liues amidft the honours, greatnes, and dignities of this world.

The fecond is in a fpirituall perfon, who defireth to ferue God, and this maketh him to feeke fweetnes, confolation and light, hauing a defire to ferue God.

The third is in perfós that haue made fome progreffe and are aduaunced in the feruice of our Lord, which is fuch that with the fame, they mingle a defire to profit greatly, and to ftriue for perfection.

Therfore great watchfulnes & heed is neceffary, to be able to know it: & for this end, it is needfull to examine very exaƈtly thy interiour, and to weigh well, whether fuch a defire be
with

with paine and anxiety, or not, and
when he findeth it to be with afflictiõ
and trouble, the perſon may be aſſured it is ſelfe-loue, and it is the more
ſubtill, in that there increaſeth with
this payne, a greater deſire of perfection. Now he that will profit indeed
muſt be wary to take away the hinderance, which is ſelf-loue, and to hope
alwaies in God, and to haue a firme
confidence, that vnto whom almighty God giueth ſuch a deſire, he will alſo giue ſtrength and meanes to bring
them to perfection, when it ſhallbe
expedient for his honour and glory.

And we muſt not think that for a-
ny diligence the ſoule can performe,
ſhe can ariue therunto, but rather
with a ſincere ſubmiſſion vnto God,
and with an operation as it were in-
ſenſible, ſhe ſhall come to haue the ac-
compliſhing of her deſire. And ſo in
this eſtate, ſhe muſt be as a little infant that ſucketh, whoſe operations
are of that quality, that they giue ioy
and conſolation to the creature, and

this

this for the innocency & purity which
is in them, which maketh such creatures, not only agreable to the Creator, but also to those that behould thē,
euen so a soule that would be depriued of proper loue, ought in this māner to imitate such actes, that is to say,
that euen as a litle infant desireth neither this, nor that, but only that which
maintaineth his life, to wit, milke, &
this without any selfe respect, euen so
a soule ought to do the like, that is to
say, to desire only that which giueth
her life which is God himselfe, and
with how much the greater sincerity,
fidelity, & constancy she seeketh God,
in the interiour of her soule, so much
the more she maketh herselfe agreeable and pleasing to his diuine Maiesty.

THE

THE CONDITIONS
that a soule ought to haue to per-
forme that which hath bene
specified, are these that
follow.

1. THE first is to desire to be euen
as perfect as God would haue
her , and when, & in the manner he pleaseth .

2 .   To take avvay all hinderances that may any vvay impeach
the execution of such a desire in
her, and endeauour that there should
not be any thing betvvene God, and
her, no not God himselfe , in regard
of the pleasure , and contentment that
is accustomed to spring of the knovv-
ledg and feeling that she hath of God
himselfe : for although that the sayd
pleasure , and contentment be not e-
uill, nor any sinne , yet notvvithstanding it hindereth, so that the disapro-
priation doth not ariue to his perfection. Therfore if somtimes the soule
take contentment or pleasure in her

F 4   selfe

selfe , and remaine busied in creatures
vnder the shadow and pretence of the
Creator; she putteth God himselfe as
a hinderance , betwene him and her
soule , and disuniteth him from the
same, for the respect she hath of that
which proceedeth from his diuinity,
or is appertaining vnto him.

3.   Not to take care , or be to much
grieued if she attain not to that height
of perfection, vnto vvhich she findeth
herselfe called; for God is infinitely
pleased to see a soule in paine for his
diuine loue , the Kingly prophet Da-
uid hauing said so much in his Psalme
90. *Cū ipso sum in tribulatione*: that is to
say, I am with him that is in tribulatiō.
For the interiour tribulations make
a soule more capable then the exteriour , to receaue particuler graces from
God; yea somtimes so great, as cannot
be thought or imagined . Therfore a
soule ought to take great heed , that
she doe not grieue or torment herself,
if she attaine not to the top of the perfection so much desired; for that som-
tymes God giueth great perfection ,
                                      and

and yet with the same a soule shall not be so agreeable to his diuine maiesty, as another that hath it not, but do on their part all that possibly they can to haue it. For hauing the said perfection she vvill haue a satisfaction, and contentment in herselfe, the vvhich although it be good, it will not be so pleasing to our Lord, as the paine & affliction that a soule suffereth for his loue: but vvith this paine and trouble she ought to be wholy conformed to his diuine will, vvithout disquiet, and not to separate herselfe any thing at al from the loue of God, for otherwise it vvilbe selfe loue.

THE EFFECTS
of self-loue.

THis self loue, although it be called in this manner, ought rather neuertheles to be called wāt of loue to our selues, hatred, death, a self venome or poyson: for that it hath no regard, nor respect, eyther to life or health, to body or soule, nor to any other
F 5   thing

thing: it esteemeth of nothing but what
it affecteth, it regardeth not God himselfe. This selfe loue was first in Lucifer when he made greater esteeme of
his owne excellency, then to be with
God in Paradise, wherby he incurred
presently death vnto himselfe, to wit,
to be separated from God: the like also
happeneth to a soule, for it separateth
it from God, maketh it become insē-
sible, taking from her the light of rea-
sō, to be opiniatiue, churlish, & void of
ciuility. This selfe loue is like vnto the
hearb called Dogs-tooth, which being
not rooted out, commeth by litle &
litle to haue such force, that it marreth
all other hearbs, that are neere vnto
it: euen so, if this selfeloue be not taken away and rooted out of our hart,
it will take such increase in our soule,
that it will spoile and corrupt all vertues and graces that are in the same;
for not only it corrupteth the vertues
that we haue gotten by our industry;
but also those that we haue receiued in
Baptisme, & in the other Sacraments.
It doth also the same in our soules, as
                                    the

the opilations or obſtructions doe in
our bodies which are the cauſes of infinite diſeaſes. It maketh a man proud
and high minded, and afterwards ca-
ſteth him into the depth of deſpaire.
It giueth him a preſuptuous ſtrength,
and hope to doe what he will, and afterwards makes him vnable, and cold
in the ſeruice of God. It clotheth the
ſoule, and coloureth it with diuers co-
lours vnder the pretence of ſanctity,
afterwardes deſpoileth it & maketh it
naked of the meanes that might bring
her to her Creator. It is a venome by
which the ſoule becommeth ſenſeleſſe,
and is ruined and deſtroied. It is like
vnto the moſt hurtfull venome of the
Aſpe : it gnaweth and conſumeth
without being perceaued, and inchaū-
teth and bewitcheth in ſuch ſort, that
ſhe knoweth not what ſhe doth, nor
what ſhe would ; but paſſing from
one thing to another, ſhe tormenteth
herſelfe, and not being able to come
to what ſhe deſireth, ſhe grieueth, fret-
teth, and pyneth away ; and if any coū-
ſell her for her help, comfort, and pro-

fit

fit, fhe remayneth as a fenfeleffe bodie
not apprehending any thing, like to
one that had no life: finally the orna-
méts that the forfaid felfe-loue giueth
vnto a foule, are thefe that follow .

First it maketh it vnlike vnto God &
like to Lucifer:it caufeth it to be hurtfull vnto others and difpleafing to herfelfe. It maketh it a veffell of contumely, or fea of iniquity . A foule infe-
&ed therwith may be likned to a fhip
that is expofed to the waues, and tem-
pefts of the fea, that is fhaken with
all fortes of windes ; like vnto a ftinking water, a barraine ground that
produceth no kind of fruit that is pleafant, an infe&ed carren, and in a word
it is like an vnbridled and vntamed
horfe; but which is moft of all, fuch a
foule deceaueth thofe that fhe con-
uerfeth withall, for fhe fheweth herfelfe as though fhe were full of vertue,
and holines, and hideth inwardly the
qualities of a venomous ferpent.

A

A DESCRIPTION
of selfe-loue.

SELFE-loue may be figured, and represếted, as a man without eyes, and notwithstanding hath foure, but none for God, but for himselfe: with two he seeth, & with other two forseeth only that which is for his cõmodity.

He hath no eares to vnderstand the voice of God that soũdeth mediatly, or immediatly, to wit, he is not attentiue, when he is excited inwardly to know his defaultes, & imperfections, but he hath 6. eares to appropriat any thing to himself: with two he heareth his owne prayses, with two others he harkeneth vnto that which may augment this selfe loue, and with the other two he is watchfull and attentiue, that nothing be said against him. He hath three hartes, and notwithstanding he hath not one that may bring him any profit, for the good of his soule, or

wherby

wherby to come to perfection, for he
hath not any affectiō, taſt, or feeling of
good. The firſt hart is for that which
concerneth his exteriour, or interiour
commodity in regard of his body.

The ſecond is for ſuch thinges as
he doth negotiate with others, to the
end the world may haue him in good
reputation.

The third maketh him to ſhew a
mild, and gracious countenance to be
beloued of all, hauing his lookes very
humble, his words faire, and well placed, outwardly an angell, but inwardly a rauening wolfe; in ſumme, ſeeking no other thing thē to pleaſe himſelfe.

HOVV SELFE-LOVE
entreth, and intrudeth it ſelfe
into all things

THis ſelfe loue is moſt ſubtile,
and hideth it ſelfe, entring and
intruding it ſelfe into all thinges,
euen vnto the Sacraments. Firſt cauſing

ſing perſons to frequent them for the
proper guſt they find therin.

Secondly to be wel eſteemed off by
others ; & alſo to couer ſome defectes,
it thruſteth it ſelf,& entreth in the ſame
manner, in hearing the word of God
for tne pleaſure they take therin. It entreth into holy Orders, when they are
receaued or vſed for vanity , for ſome
commodity, ambition, or other euill
deſignement. It thruſteth it ſelfe into
marriages,whē they marry for to ſatiſ-
fy their concupiſcence,& appetites. It
intrudeth it ſelfe alſo into the practiſe
of vertues, procuring that great paine
and trauell be imployed in it, without
hauing any good , right, or ſincere
intention for the glory of God , but
rather for ſome other reſpect. It thruſteth it ſelfe , and entreth into the exerciſe of Prayer, pretending to receaue therin taſt, light, & feeling , vnder pretence to be vnited vnto God,
and in doing this , the perſon ſo infected, ſeeketh himſelfe. A ſigne of this
is , that when the conſolations are taken away and loſt, he doth not per-
ſeuere

seuere in prayer. It hideth it selfe vnder humility, and seemeth vile, and
abie&t : but vvhen others say so much
he is troubled : and vndoubtedly this
is a true signe of selfe-loue It will haue
also part in obedience, for such a one
pretendeth very willingly to accept,
whatsoeuer is commaunded him; but
soone after he putteth so many excuses and reasons, that he hindereth the
effe&t of the same, & dischargeth himselfe of what is commaunded. It putteth it selfe into the desire of bearing
the crosse with our Sauiour Christ,
first inciting a desire with a great gree-
dines of the sharpest, and most bitter
things that may be, as we see womē
great with child couet to eat strange
thinges, as coales, earth, and the like
impertinent stuffe, and yet this desire
of the crosse shalbe for other ends, &
motiues, then for the loue of God.
Secondly it entreth into the desire to
satisfy for sinnes, and to increase in
merit, when the soule remaineth and
perseuereth on the crosse, saying, that
she will satisfy the more for her offences

ces , and by it she shall remaine lesse tyme in Purgatory , or els that there will so much the lesse rest to be purged, and merit wilbe increased therby: without all doubt these pretences proceed of selfe-loue .

Thirdly, it thrusteth it selfe to the bearing of a crosse , and suffering of afflictions for vain glory; as well knowing that commonly such persons as are much troubled , and afflicted , are very much admired of the world , & are held for Saints, in hauing such trialls, and are thought to be greatly pleasing vnto God. It entreth also by a certain superfluous ouer great , and excessiue desire of the crosse , but it is for the pleasure that one taketh oftentimes in the same crosse, in which selfe-loue much delighted.

P R O-

PROPERTIES
of a soule infected with selfe-loue.

SELFE loue robbeth from God, what appertaineth vnto him, for it stealeth and taketh from him his honour, by seeking to attribute the same vnto himself, as the Pharisie robbed our Lord of his honour, whē he said, *non sum sicut ceteri hominum*, I am not like vnto other men.

First this loue maketh the soule vn-like vnto God, being a most simple obiect, an infinite purity; selfe-loue maketh the soule double, crafty, and dissembling, and causeth it to seeme o-ther then it is.

Secondly it maketh him like vnto the diuell, for euen as the diuell is neuer content, nor reposeth; so the like miseries doth selfe loue cause in the soule, for it causeth much vnqui-etnes, and many troubles in her, not being able to find any repose
or

or contentment . It maketh it a ly-
ar, and an enemy to truth, and by
this meanes she becommeth hatefull
vnto others; for that such qualities are
insupportable: moreouer it maketh it
continually fretting and vnquiet, for
neuer finding any repose , and not da-
ring to desire death by reason of this
selfe loue, she tormenteth & afflicteth
herselfe without ceasing . It bringeth
her also to be a vessell of contumely,
for that to satisfy herselfe she doth e-
uen her best actions, desiring prayers,
the Sacraments, and such like things,
hauing for a foundation of all this her
selfe loue. And thus the works become defiled, foule and infected with
this selfe loue, and the soule by this
meanes is a sea of iniquity: for the bottome of her imperfections not being
able to be found , she is as a sea without bottome, that is moued and troubled with contrary winds, & swolne
with meruailous great, fearefull , and
horrible waues, being angry and euer
opposing herselfe against those that
would affoard her any help or remedy .

dy. She is also like vnto a ship, expofed
to the tēpefts & raging of the fea, for
this foule sailing in the fea of felf-loue,
euen as a ship in the fea, fo is she com-
bated on euery fide, making ship-
wrack for a fmall matter. She may alfo
be compared to a ftinking vvater, for
she runneth on euery fide (as vvater
that hath no ftay) to feeke if she can
find contentment, but by reafon of
her imperfections she is very noyfome
and yeldeth an euill fauour vnto thofe
that are pure, and cleane. She refembleth alfo a barraine ground, that produceth nothing but thornes, thiftles,
& other fuch vnfauoury weeds, fpoi-
ling all the fruit of good workes. She
is like vnto a ftinking carren, for this
felfe-loue infecteth the foule and maketh her ferue him as food to a rauen,
and aftervvards to become a prey and
repaft to that infernall fiend whome
she refembleth. Breifly this loue thus
qualified, is as an vntamed horfe without bit, or bridle, it vvill not be ruled
by any perfon, nor containe it felfe,
neither by counfell, nor by fkilful aduife,

uiſe, but it maketh the ſoule remaine
as rooted in her proper ſenſe, and ſelf
iudgment, vvherby ſhe becommeth
incorrigible: & this happeneth ſome-
times to ſome ſpirituall perſon, vnder
colour of ſanƈtity, vvhich is very
hardly cured.

This forſaid ſelf-loue ſpringeth of
the delight that the creature hopeth to
enioy in thoſe things ſhe ſeeketh, and
which do appertaine vnto her, and it
groweth to that paſſe, that ſhe eſtemeth
not of her life, nor of any other thing
els, in reſpeƈt of attayning to what ſhe
ſo liketh. It proceedeth alſo of the nature wounded & corrupted in her i-
raſcible and concupiſcible powers, and
euill habits, and cuſtomes which haue
gotten root in the ſoule. And this is
vnderſtood, not only of the firſt kind
of ſelf-loue which is common & familiar
to worldly perſons, but alſo of the ſecond, wherwith oftentimes ſpirituall
perſons are intangled, the which may
be called ſelf-loue, for the taſt, and
pleaſure that they ſeeke in ſpirituall
thinges. It is vnderſtood alſo of the
third

third kind of self-loue in spirituall persons, who are already aduaunced and
profited in the way of vertue, which
may be compared to the poyson of the
diamōd, that gnaweth a creature, interiourly by litle & litle, but it leaueth
no exteriour signe, as other poysōs do:
so this proper loue gnaweth oftentymes inwardly the conscience, but it
leaueth no mark or signe in the soule,
but killeth it, and bringeth it in the
end to death, & damnation. It is a very
euident signe of the forsaid self-loue,
when our Lord hath giuen any particuler grace to a soule, and when it
pleaseth him to depriue her of it, she
falleth into great griefe and sadnes.

The root of this forsaid selfe loue lieth hid vnder the colour of faygned
holines, and guideth the soule   a very strait, and narrow way, and maketh it appeare, to those that conuerse
which such a person, that the way to
serue God is very strait, and more difficult, then in truth it is. It engendreth
a great wearines of sanctity aswell in
the parties that haue it, as in the per-
                                    sons

ſons that conuerſe with them, which
is no true holines . It exciteth a great
meruaile, and an aſtoniſhment with
vnquietnes, which procureth to the
parties a diſguſt and confuſiō, in ſeing
that they cānot arriue to that perfeſtion and holines, which they ſee in o-
thers, wherby they remayne without
repoſe, which is a great ſigne that this
holines proceedeth of ſelfe loue . And
ſhe that wrote this diſcourſe witneſ-
ſeth to haue proued & found this many tymes in herſelfe, to wit, that in
thinking on the ſanſtity of ſome ſuch
perſon, ſhe much meruailed, but notwithſtanding ſhe did not fall into vnquietnes and confuſion .

R E M E D I E S
againſt ſelfe-loue.

1 . **FIRST** the ſoule infeſted
Herewith muſt ſeeke to haue
a perſon very much enlight-
ned by God, that hath the diſcretion
of pirits, with whom ſhe muſt confer
of her troubles & deſires, and according

ding to his iudgment esteeme herselfe
to be sick, and to haue need of help,
as in truth she hath, and is not able to
help her selfe.

2. Secondly she must seeke to mortify all her desires and affections, as-
vvell of those thinges that are good,
and holy, as of those that are indifferent, and not to run after them, especially, when she is most prouoked
vnto them, and for this effect it will
serue her much to lay open her hart to
her spirituall father, and suffer herselfe
to be guided, and conducted by him.

3. Thirdly the remedy is to thinke
that all thinges, how good and holy
soeuer they be, are not alwayes pleasing to God, but only those that come
from him, and are required by him,
And by this we may know, that they
come frō him when the said things do
not moue vs nor lift vs vp vnto pride
in hauing them, nor torment & afflict
vs in hauing them not, but bring with
them a peace and tranquillity to the
soule: in such sort, that she remayneth in as great repose in the executiō
of

of them, as if ſhe did not execute them at all.

4. The fourth remedy is to conſider, that to accompliſh ſuch deſires of this ſelf-loue, is to contemne God, and to contradiƈt, and be oppoſite to the diuine will, for ſo much as diuine loue, is altogeather contrary to ſelfe loue, and all our aƈtions that we are induced vnto by it, are contrary to the bleſſed will of God, and by that meanes we become oppoſite, and contrary vnto him.

5. The fifth remedy belongeth to the ſpirituall father, who to take away, and cleere the ſoule from all ſelfe loue, in all that ſhe pretendeth in her aƈtions, and deſires muſt firſt ſeeke all the meanes to penetrate into her hart, that is to gaine her good opiniõ and eſtimation, and to be gratefull vnto her; & afterwards he muſt begin with great ſweetnes to apply his remedies, and ſo to cure and heale her: which muſt not be done in ſuch open manner that ſhe may perceaue it, but with ſome kind of diſſimulation, and

G   as

as it were in ieſt, making her to doe
all thinges contrary to that ſhe diſpo-
ſeth of, and deſireth to doe, and taking
away ſomtymes all this againe, chan-
ging it into ſome other like thing : as
for example, if the ſaid perſon be de-
ſirous to goe vnto one place of recreation, to make her goe to another, ſomtymes alſo not taking them away altogeather, but correcting them, as if
ſhe would mortify herſelfe with long
diſciplines, to make her to vſe ſhort, for
ſeldome it doth profit to withſtand
proper loue altogeather at one blow,
as to forbid her wholy diſciplines, except it be to a perſon already aduaunced in the way of perfection, and in
the exerciſe therof. And as this his dexterity ought to proceed of charity, &
loue ſo alſo ought ſhe to be ruled with
the ſame loue, for ſo much as in ſuch
cures and ſicknes, ſeuerity profiteth
nothing, by reaſon that this ſelfe-loue
is ſweet & gracious, and maketh the
ſoule very tender and delicate ſo that
if ſhe be vſed with ſharpnes & rough-
nes, ſhe entreth preſently into diſdain,

flieth

flieth and abhorreth the cure . And by
this may be feene, that felfe-loue is
healed with loue, and by loue .

This fwetnes is moft neceffary in
fuperiours, and principally when they
treat with thofe vnder their charge, of
thinges appertayning to the fuperiour
part, and fpirit : for ordinarily in this
affaire all the euill proceedeth of this
roote, and feuerity procureth anger,
and difdaine, and hindreth much: and
moreouer the Phifitian of felfe-loue
muft note, that he ought to be continually diligent, and not to abandon the
cure, but to doe as a Phifitian doth ,
who hath one-grieuoufly fick in his
charge, for he vifiteth often his patient, and many tymes feeleth his pulfe,
and neuer abandoneth nor leaueth
him , vntill he perceaue that he is in
better eftate, and that he beginneth to
amend .

He muft alfo note, that there be
two fortes of perfons that are fick of
this felfe loue, fome of them are as it
were in a confuming feauer, the euill
wherof hath already very much pene-

G 2   trated

trated into the inward part ; and although oftentimes they are incurable,
or at the leaft very hard to be cured ,
yet notwithftanding, he muft not alwaies defpaire of them, but muft performe in their behalfe what the faid
corporall Phifitian doth to thofe that
hath the forfaid difeafe, to wit, to performe on his part , whatfoeuer he can,
and to leaue the reft vnto God ; but
he muft take great heed , that he doe
not beare himfelfe to harfh and to au-
ftere, for that would be very doma-
geable , and pernicious .

The others that are ficke are fuch,
and of fuch an humor, as they may be
healed ,and although it be needfull to
vfe great fwetnes, & dexterity in their
behalfe , as hath bene faid before , and
that there is great difficulty in the cure,
yet notwithftanding he muft not defpaire , by reafon of the difficulty that
he perceaueth in the beginning ; for
the caufe of this difficulty is , that this
proper loue , doth fo much blind the
foule , that it doth not permit her to
fee clearly her faultes, and imperfections

ons : and therfore she not acknowledging herselfe to be sicke, the euill can
hardly be cured, so that one ought to
imploy all his care, and industry to
make her to enter into this knowledg,
which in the end wil serue very much
for her remedy and cure.

First the said spirituall father must
take great heed that he speake not any
thing of self-loue, and that must be
shunned from the beginning, least the
infirme should be too much dismayed
and fall into too much feare: but he
must a far off put before her, and
cause her to practise the exercise of difappropriation, depriuing her first of
some thinges, not very difficult vnto
her, afterwardes make her returne to
herselfe, and cause her to know how
she was hindred in this loue, although
in chiding her, he ought to say nothing
that may contristate her, or to seeme
to blame her, but rather by little and
little make her know her euill; notwithstanding when she knoweth it, or
when she is cured, then he must make
her vnderstand, how great, and dan-

G 3   gerous

gerous it was, for he muſt cóport himſelfe in this behalfe, as a guid doth in a
iourney, who being to paſſe ſome dangerous ſtrait, ſaith nothing to the paſſē-
gers of the perill and daunger, but only encourageth them to follow him,
& afterwardes hauing paſſed the ſtrait,
hath no more care, nor looketh back
vnto it; euen ſo, thoſe that treat with
ſuch kind of perſons, ought to behaue
themſelues dexterouſly without making them to thinke of the difficulty that they ſhall haue to mortify
the ſaid ſelfe-loue, ſomtimes ſpeaking
to them in parables and ſimilitudes, in
a third perſon, ſomtimes by good
counſell, making them to vnderſtand
and to come to the knowledg of their
defectes, then with ſweetnes, and taking euer ſome good occaſió to make
them to returne, and enter into themſelues.

Whileſt I was a writing a copy of
this booke, our Lord made this vertuous Dame that compoſed it, to vnderſtand, that ſhe ſhould aduertiſe me
of this that followeth, that I might ſet
                                                    it

it downe in the end of this worke,
to wit, that as there is an Angell appointed ouer proper loue to repreſſe
it, and to fight againſt it : ſo there is
another ouer the loue of God, to conſerue, increaſe, and augment it, who
from the beginning of their creation
were deputed to this functiō, the one,
and the other, not paſſing further then
their charge. S. *Gabriel* was deputed
ouer diuine loue, by the meanes
wherof he was choſen to be the meſ-
ſenger of the ſacred myſtery of the Incarnation of the Sonne of God, a
worke of moſt ſingūlar loue of Almighty God towards mankind, vnto whom it was eſpecially reuealed in
heauē by the moſt Bl. Trinity, when
the diuine perſons made their actes of
reciprocall loue. S. *Michael* was alſo
appointed ouer proper loue; & therfore when Lucifer rebelled in heauen
againſt God, ſeeking to be like to the
moſt high, & equalling himſelfe with
him, he was ordeyned by our Lord to
reſiſt him, as he that had a great zeale
of diuine loue, contrary to this ſelfe
loue,

loue. Our Lord then reuealed this secret to this holy Dame, & said vnto
her : Aduertise thy spirituall father,
that he may learne, that when any one
would heale a soule, infected vvith
selfe loue, he demaund my ayd, and
succour by the prayers and intercessi-
on of S. *Michael* the *Archangel*, and
when any soule shalbe touched, & sur-
prized with diuine loue, it is needfull
that she implore the fauour of S. *Gabriel*, to the end, that by this meanes
she may more easily attaine vnto the
soueraigne perfection of the said loue
of God.

A

A

SVPPLY OF

THIS
ABRIDGMENT

for to afcend vnto a moft high
and great Perfection.

THE perfection prefup-
pofed of all the eftates
before declared, euen
vnto this prefent, which
confifteth in an vtter
forfaking of all preten-
ces whatfoeuer, and not to pretend
any other thing, but God onely, in
a moft excellent, and a moft perfect
manner, in all our actions, whereby
we may attayne vnto a moft high
per-

perfe&ion, which confifteth in the ex-
amen following , diftinguifhed into
feauen points.

1.   The firft is , when the foule ap-
prehendeth any trouble or afflidtion,
that of new is prefented vnto her.
For that then by the fuggeftion of
the inferiour , or infirme part , the ap-
prehenfion of fuch a croffe is accuftomed to be very vehement : and vvith
this, a thoufand exaggerations wilbe
prefented , that will caufe it to appeare
more violent, wherby the foule is accuftomed to take this afflidtion vvith
much difficulty, and many repugnances

To remedy this, and to prouide for
it throughly, it is neceffary that the fuperiour part of the foule , propofe all
this before her, as a Iudg doth, who before he giue his fentence , harkneth to
the reafons of both parties , prouided
alwaies that fhe be not moued any
thing with their reafons, but that fhe
remaine without paffion or any kind
of alteration , fufpending her iudgement, vntill fhe find out what may
be

be according to reaſon, and that ſhe
may the better vnderſtãd it, theſe two
meanes will ayd her. The one is,that
ſhe enter into herſelfe, and conſider
how almighty God knoweth, and ſeeth all her troubles, and whatſoeuer
ſhe endureth, and therfore ſhe ought
to remit it wholy into his handes, to
diſpoſe therof as he ſeeth moſt expedient. The ſecond is to conſider, & be-
lieue aſſuredly, that euen as the diuine bounty deſireth nothing but our
good, euen ſo his diuine prouidence
(which is hid from vs,not being permitted vnto vs to ſeeke too curiouſly
into it) knoweth very well how to
prouide and remedy all in tyme, and
manner, as it ſhall ſeeme beſt vnto
him, and not as beſt liketh vs, nor
as it may beſt pleaſe vs. Of this ſuſ-
penſion ,and repoſe of ſpirit followeth
two things; the firſt that ſhe putteth
away, and reiecteth all the hinderances, and troubles, and the deceytes
that might happen by this apprehen-
ſion: and ſecondly it will follow, that
ſhe ſhal come to conceaue a true,pure,

ſin-

sincere, & mature apprehension of all her affaires.

The second point is, that when the soule is come to receaue, and accept this afliction, as comming from God.

REMEDIES.

SHE must not rest herselfe heere, or permit herselfe to accept of it, as often many soules are accustomed to doe, to wit, basely with an infinit number of difficultyes, of excuses, and seeking of themselues, but she must accept therof in a high manner and perfectly, to wit, from the hand of God, with a perfect submission, & resignation to his diuine will, resigning herselfe wholy into his handes, and possession, surmounting all difficulties hovv great foeuer may be presented vnto her.

3.   The third point is to know how the soule ought to behaue herselfe in the behalfe of the inferiour part, to wit, in afflictions, troubles, and motions, concerning paines, sicknes, or
other

other corporall accidents, that are accustomed to proceed of these afflictions, for the repugnance, and contra-
riety that nature findeth therin.

REMEDIES.

REASON & the superiour part of
the soule ought by the influence
of grace, and interiour recollection, to impart, and send forth force
and strength of vertue, aswell into the
parts of the soule, as into the weake
and sensible partes of the body; in
such sort, that they also accept of
these torments, and doe accord togeather, and that the superiour powers doe remoue certaine hardnes,
difficulties, rages, and such other
disorders, as spring and proceed ordinarily of those repugnances, and
contrarieties, which they haue bene
accustomed to feele in the like incom-
brances; and the foresaid superiour
part of the soule, ought to procure,
that in the vertue of this interiour
recollection, they haue in themselues,

a

a certaine promptnes to suffer all the
foresaid afflictions, euen as readily,
as if in place of these paines, there
were presented vnto them some thing
agreable, commodious, or much to
their contentment: by the same force,
and vertue she ought to offer it, and
returne it vnto God, accepting it only
in him, and for him.

4. The fourth point, is to know
in what manner the superiour part,
must suffer with the inferiour, and
with the exteriour senses, in the repugnances, and contrarieties which
they feele, as hath bene said before.

REMEDIES.

THE superiour part ought to doe
all, that hath bene said before
in the behalfe of the inferiour,
and weakest partes, in such sort, that
it be not with a certaine excessiue
violence, which may cause them wholy to loose their strength, and vigour,
                                          or

or ſo, as may trouble, or make the
ſoule puſillanimous and fearefull, or
els vtterly vnable to ſupport ſo great a
blow; but ſhe ought for this cauſe
ſomthing to ſuffer with them, and
encourage them with all the reaſons
ſhe can imagine, and ſhe muſt doe all
this with the greateſt diſcretion that
ſhe can poſſibly, in giuing now and
then ſome relaxation vnto their tra-
uailes, and afflictions, and in ſeeking
the moſt conuenient remedies that
ſhe can aduiſe herſelfe of. Euen as
one that would haue a horſe, or any
other beaſt to ſerue his turne, will
giue him more meat, to the end he
may be ſtrong, and able to trauaile
more when there is need. And when
by reaſon of diuine ſubtraction ſhe
cannot vſe the force of any act of conſolation, or rayſing vp of her mind,
ſhe ought to repoſe in this, and procure the partes that are inferiour, to
repoſe in the will of God, and this
by meanes of the diuine conformity, which will bring much more
true and ſtrengthning conſolation, although

though it doth not feeme fo.

5. The fift point is, how fhe ought to comport herfelfe with felfe-loue in this cafe, or the like.

REMEDIES.

SELFE Loue is accuftomed to pretend and feeke in all thinges her owne intereft, and particuler commoditie directly, or indirectly; and it doth fo alfo in this, vnder pretence of many good reafons, yea euen of vertues, and purpofeth many thinges that are not to the purpofe; and for this caufe the foule with the purity of a right intention ought to difcouer by the light of the loue of God, all his deceipts, and oppofe herfelfe againft this felfe-loue very freely, and effectually; and by the force of a pure and cleane loue, fhe ought to reiect all particuler and felfe refpect, and follow purely that which God fhall infpire and teach her.

6. The fixt point is, how that the
fu-

superiour part ought to anfwere to the
propofitions or offers that our Lord
will make vnto her, concerning thefe
paines, and afflictions, or other greater.

REMEDIES.

AFTER this that hath byn aboue
faid, our Lord is accuftomed
to make many propofitions to
the foule : as for example, that he will
fend her many other afflictions, or
els make her endure this prefent affliction a long tyme, yea that we will
caufe her to fuffer euen the paines of
hell ; and then ought fhe with great
promptnes to be wholy refigned vnto
God . He alfo is accuftomed to giue
the choice of two kindes of afflictions
for her to accept of one . And in this
cafe rayfing and fixing the eyes of her
foule wholy in the perfect loue of
God, with a meruailous purity, fhe
ought to make her election in God,
and this choice muft be alwaies of that
which

which will redound moſt to his honour and glory .

7 .   The ſeauenth is , in what manner ſhe ought to behaue herſelf , that
ſhe may vſe all her powers in the execution of this affaire , or of this affliction , and of all that which ſhalbe
neceſſary ,to come to the height of this
perfection .

REMEDIES .

FOR as much as ordinarily in the
exerciſing of all theſe thinges , it
is neceſſary that all the powers ,
& faculties of the ſoule concurre therunto , to put it duly in execution ; ſhe
ought fully to reſolue with herſelfe
to obſerue all that ſhe hath deliberated
vpon in ſuch ſort , that aſwell in generall, as in particuler, ſhe may perfectly
accompliſh , and put in execution all
this that ſhe hath already choſen , and
reſolued to doe in the preſent affliction , or in any other thing : and ſhe
ought to take heed diligently to correct

rect the faultes that may happen in
the execution, eyther by reaſon of
her imagination, and repreſentation
of afflictions, or of the vnderſtanding,
or of the will, or of all the other powers. And thus the ſoule that is perfect, ſhall become much more perfect : and all this is a diſpoſition vnto
the ſtate, that rendereth the ſoule wholy diuine.

A T A-

A
TABLE OF
THE
CHAPTERS,
AND
principall Contents of this
Booke .

THE TABLE.

THE

THE LADDER
of Perfection.

A

FINIS.

*For Product Safety Concerns and Information please contact
our EU representative GPSR@taylorandfrancis.com Taylor & Francis
Verlag GmbH, Kaufingerstraße 24, 80331 München, Germany*

T - #0053 - 270225 - C0 - 186/123/16 [18] - CB - 9780754631460 - Gloss Lamination